CLASSICS IN EDUCATION
Lawrence A. Cremin, General Editor

☆ ☆ ☆

THE REPUBLIC AND THE SCHOOL
Horace Mann on the Education of Free Men
Edited by Lawrence A. Cremin

AMERICAN IDEAS ABOUT ADULT EDUCATION
1710–1951
Edited by C. Hartley Grattan

DEWEY ON EDUCATION
Introduction and Notes by Martin S. Dworkin

THE SUPREME COURT AND EDUCATION
(Revised and enlarged)
Edited by David Fellman

INTERNATIONAL EDUCATION
A Documentary History
Edited by David G. Scanlon

CRUSADE AGAINST IGNORANCE
Thomas Jefferson on Education
Edited by Gordon C. Lee

CHINESE EDUCATION UNDER COMMUNISM
Edited by Chang-tu Hu

CHARLES W. ELIOT AND POPULAR EDUCATION
Edited by Edward A. Krug

WILLIAM T. HARRIS ON EDUCATION
(in preparation)
Edited by Martin S. Dworkin

THE *EMILE* OF JEAN JACQUES ROUSSEAU
Selections
Translated and Edited by William Boyd

THE AGE OF THE ACADEMIES
Edited by Theodore R. Sizer

HEALTH, GROWTH, AND HEREDITY
G. Stanley Hall on Natural Education
Edited by Charles E. Strickland and Charles Burgess

TEACHER EDUCATION IN AMERICA
A Documentary History
Edited by Merle L. Borrowman

THE EDUCATED WOMAN IN AMERICA
Selected Writings of Catharine Beecher,
Margaret Fuller, and M. Carey Thomas
Edited by Barbara M. Cross

EMERSON ON EDUCATION
Selections
Edited by Howard Mumford Jones

ECONOMIC INFLUENCES UPON EDUCATIONAL
PROGRESS IN THE UNITED STATES, 1820–1850
By Frank Tracy Carlton
Foreword by Lawrence A. Cremin

QUINTILIAN ON EDUCATION
Selected and Translated by William M. Smail

ROMAN EDUCATION FROM CICERO
TO QUINTILIAN
By Aubrey Gwynn, S.J.

HERBERT SPENCER ON EDUCATION
Edited by Andreas M. Kazamias

JOHN LOCKE'S *OF THE CONDUCT*
OF THE UNDERSTANDING
Edited by Francis W. Garforth

STUDIES IN EDUCATION DURING THE
AGE OF THE RENAISSANCE, 1400–1600
By William Harrison Woodward
Foreword by Lawrence Stone

Sir Thomas Elyot's
The Book
Named the Governor

Abridged and Edited by
JOHN M. MAJOR

CLASSICS IN

No. 40

EDUCATION

TEACHERS COLLEGE PRESS
TEACHERS COLLEGE, COLUMBIA UNIVERSITY
NEW YORK

Foreword

The Renaissance civility book constitutes a fascinating genre in the literature of educational philosophy. As John E. Mason made clear in his admirable explication of the genre, *Gentlefolk in the Making* (1935), it took several forms at least during that turbulent period between 1480 and 1640, when England crossed over the threshold of modernity. First, there was the book of parental advice, frequently informal in tone and almost always filled with the commonplaces of proverbial wisdom—the *Basilikon Doron* (1599) of James I is a splendid example. Then, there was the manual of polite conduct, somewhat more formal in character and almost always more systematic in argument—Baldassare Castiglione's *The Courtier* (1528) is an excellent case in point. And, finally, there was the treatise on politics, which commonly included strictures on education as an essential element in the conduct of a just state—Sir Thomas More's *Utopia* (1516) is the best-known instance. In a sense, all such books did double duty as expositions of educational theory and policy: they set forth standards of character and conduct, thereby helping to define the ends of education; and they indicated the processes and agencies through which that education would proceed.

Sir Thomas Elyot's *The Book Named the Governor* (1531) was one of the more influential of these treatises. Addressed primarily to the newly self-conscious gentry of Henrician England, it set out to persuade them that a liberal education is requisite to the responsible exercise of political power. It was, as Professor Major points out, a tractate of education, a courtesy manual, a handbook of moral philosophy, and a treatise on politics. And by at least one canon it must be judged an outstanding success: it went through numerous editions in its own right, and it served as a model for a half-dozen other works as significant as Sir Humphrey Gilbert's *Queen Elizabeth's Academy* (*c.* 1572) and Thomas Fuller's *The Holy State, and the Profane State* (1642). Moreover, together with these, it ultimately proved persuasive; for the fact is that the gentry did take unto themselves the ideal of gentility, in the process transforming both English education and the English state. And that, incidentally, is no small tribute to the first systematic work on education published in the English language.

LAWRENCE A. CREMIN

Preface

Sir Thomas Elyot's *The Book Named the Governor*, first published in the year 1531, belongs with that impressive company of works by learned Renaissance authors—*The Schoolmaster, The Advancement of Learning,* and *The Anatomy of Melancholy* are others that come to mind— which were conceived on a grand scale; run to great length (they ramble, too); cover a variety of topics; and are generally written in a vein of high seriousness, lightened with humor, with wit, with candor, with anecdotes galore, and with much delightful freshness of language and forthright statement. Such works spring from the noblest of aims: a desire to improve mankind through instruction in the kinds of knowledge in which their authors were expert, the imparting or sharing of which they thought vital to the well-being of humanity (especially English humanity) and of the nation or society. All are in a sense books of education, *The Governor* and *The Schoolmaster* more strictly so. But *The Governor* is many things: a tractate of education for the children of the English ruling class, deriving from Cicero's and Quintilian's works on the education of the orator, from Plutarch, and from educational writings by the Italian humanists of the fifteenth and sixteenth centuries and by Erasmus; a courtesy book like Castiglione's *The Courtier;* a *speculum principis* or prince's mirror like a host of such books going back to Isocrates' oration *To Nicocles* and coming forward to Erasmus' *The Education of a Chris-*

tian Prince; a handbook of moral philosophy like Cicero's
De officiis; a treatise of politics like More's *Utopia* or
(on a very modest scale) Plato's *Republic;* and a sub-
dictionary of new words introduced by Elyot for the necessary augmentation of the English language.

Despite such multiplicity of aims and sources and
methods, *The Governor* does have design and unity—of
a Tudor kind, at any rate. The three books that make up
the whole comprise three more or less distinct topics.
Book I treats the formal education, in the various branches
of learning—the encyclopedia—of the boy and young
man from about seven years of age to about twenty. Book
II instructs the young man, now on the threshold of his
career in government, in the qualities which go to make
up true nobility, a condition of character, conduct, deportment, appearance, and personality essential in a
good governor. Book III rounds out the pre-governing
instruction in moral philosophy by offering extended
definitions of three of the cardinal virtues—justice, fortitude, and temperance—the fourth, prudence, having
been defined, allegorically, in Book I in the chapters on
dancing; Book III considers also the higher (spiritual?)
virtues of wisdom and understanding, and concludes with
a discussion of the importance to a governor of experience
and of the giving and receiving of good counsel. (For details, the reader may consult Elyot's Table of Contents,
given below entire.) The whole thus has an architectonic
pattern, in Sidney's sense of Aristotle's term: wisdom being the end product of nature, the God-given, brought to
perfection by learning; counsel being the fruit of wisdom;
and counselors-governors being wise men who employ
their wisdom in the active life to the benefit of others.

Although *The Governor* in its entirety is about education, the part best suited to the aim of this series, CLASSICS

IN EDUCATION, and conforming to the length of other volumes in the series, is Book I, in which Elyot takes his pupil step by step through his formal education, from learning at an early age to read, speak, and write good Latin to studying at the last moral philosophy, after he has matured and after he has been prepared, through his knowledge of other subjects, to understand this weightier and more abstract discipline. The reader will thus find in Book I of this early-sixteenth-century work a treatise, near-complete in itself, on the kind of aristocratic education, strongly humanistic in its emphasis, which molded (besides many poets and men of learning) the lawyers, magistrates, justices, ambassadors, ministers, deputies, courtiers, and even monarchs who managed the affairs of England for several generations. Indeed, after allowing for such changes as the steady advance of knowledge, particularly in mathematics and the natural sciences, and the increasing numbers of noblemen's and gentlemen's children who attended schools and universities instead of being tutored at home, Sir Thomas Elyot's ideal of education, which aimed to fashion the scholar-gentleman–public servant, has prevailed even to our own century, and may be said on the whole to have served the needs of England's governments rather splendidly.

It might be added that Book I is also by all odds the most interesting of the three books of *The Governor*.

The text of the present edition is based on a copy of the first (1531) edition of *The Governor* in possession of the Henry E. Huntington Library. For the convenience of the reader, I have modernized spelling and punctuation, though out of respect for Elyot's integrity as author and his often appealing and eloquent style, I have tried to make only those changes which seemed necessary to the clarity. *The Governor* reveals its early date in the

history of Modern English prose in an occasional awk-
wardness of syntax; besides non-sentences, it contains
many very long sentences loosely strung together with
such connectives as "which," "whereof," and "for as much
as." The punctuation, consisting chiefly of virgule and
colon, and lavishly employed, serves mainly to set off
phrases and other syntactical units, secondarily for emphasis or pause. To clarify some of Elyot's longer sentences, I have had to make rather too much use of that
modern all-purpose mark, the dash; and at times I have
combined into a sentence two or more of Elyot's fragments. "Which," "whereof," and similar words often
function as demonstratives, and should be so read. In
"streamlining" the style, I hope I have not altered too
much Elyot's sentence rhythms, since of course these were
for the most part deliberate and have literary worth.
Many of the (to us) peculiarities of Elyot's style are no
doubt the result of his having followed Latin, in particular the Ciceronian, models.

If a word used by Elyot is still current, I have simply
given it its modern spelling, though I have not in this
practice been everywhere consistent, preferring, for example, "alway" to "always," "other" to "others," "at-
temptate" to "attempt," etc. Archaic and obsolete words
I have glossed in footnotes (once for each such word in
each chapter), relying for definitions on the *OED* and, occasionally, on Croft's very scholarly nineteenth-century
edition of *The Governor*.

References, allusions, and quotations abound in this
learned work of Elyot's. I have not thought it necessary
to identify them, since my version is intended for the
general reader. Readers of a more scholarly bent will
find them traced down and discussed at length in the two-
volume edition of *The Governor* by H. H. S. Croft (Lon-

don: Kegan, Paul, Trench, 1880; repr. New York: Burt Franklin, 1967).

The original text of *The Governor* (entire) may be read in Croft's edition or in the Everyman edition (edited by Foster Watson, 1907). The new Everyman edition (edited by Stanford E. Lehmberg, 1962) is in modernized spelling and punctuation.

I am grateful to the trustees of the Henry E. Huntington Library and Art Gallery for permitting me to work from their copy of the 1531 edition of *The Governor*.

J. M. M.

Contents

Sir Thomas Elyot's
The Book Named the Governor

Introduction

By JOHN M. MAJOR

Since the life of an author, especially the author of a Renaissance book on education, is always pertinent to his thought and literary expression, it seems appropriate to begin this introduction with a brief biography of Elyot, insofar as the facts of his life have come down to us.

Sir Thomas Elyot was born around the year 1490 into a family of West Country gentry.[1] His father, Sir Richard Elyot, was a jurist of distinction—Serjeant-at-Law, Justice of Assize for the Western Circuit, and Judge of the Common Pleas—a member of three Parliaments, and a considerable landowner. Thomas Elyot was thus born into the governing class, and was raised among them, many other of his relatives being also active in government in various ways.

Until entering the Middle Temple (one of the Inns of Court or law schools) around 1510, Thomas Elyot was educated at home, and very thoroughly, it would appear. Some six years *after* entering the Middle Temple, a Thomas Eliett (or Eyllyett or Elyett or Elyott)—possibly our man—entered Oxford, where he took the degrees Bachelor of Arts in 1519 and Bachelor of Civil Law in 1524. This somewhat unusual sequence is partly explained by a statement of R. W. Chambers: "most young

[1] For most of the biographical information in the following pages I am indebted to Stanford E. Lehmberg, *Sir Thomas Elyot: Tudor Humanist* (Austin: University of Texas Press, 1960).

men ambitious of distinction in civil life went straight to one of the Inns of Court" instead of attending a university; the Inns of the time were in fact virtually universities.[2] And although in *The Governor* Elyot insists that the young man complete his education in the humanities before taking up the study of law, the Oxford and Cambridge of Elyot's day, and of Milton's a century later, still settled firmly in a largely medieval curriculum, had little to offer in the way of a humanistic education. If Elyot did in fact attend Oxford at the time indicated (how ancient he must have appeared among the other undergraduates), it would have been for a reason or reasons now obscure.[3]

Despite all this legal training, there is no evidence that Elyot was ever admitted to the bar or practiced law. No doubt knowledge of the law was useful to him, however, in the various governmental offices he was to assume.

At some time during his young manhood Elyot became a protégé of Thomas Cardinal Wolsey, a friend of Sir Thomas More, and a friend and off-and-on protégé of Thomas Cromwell—each in his brief turn political ruler of England just below the king himself. In spite of, or perhaps because of, these powerful connections, Elyot never advanced to very high office or, by his reckoning, prospered materially.

[2] R. W. Chambers, *Thomas More* (London: Jonathan Cape, 1949), p. 67.

[3] Pearl Hogrefe, in *The Life and Times of Sir Thomas Elyot, Englishman* (Ames: Iowa State University Press, 1967), pp. 48–50, dismisses the theory that the author of *The Governor* attended a university, accepting as truthful his own statements on his education, and pointing out the fact that the Thomas Elyot who was enrolled at Oxford could have been any one of a half dozen persons of that name living in England at the time.

We might examine briefly at this point Elyot's association with the greatest and best of these men, More. Although in later years, after More's execution, Elyot found it necessary to deny, rather meanly, any friendship with More so close as to be considered treasonable, it is very likely true that the two men had never been intimate friends. Nowhere in the extensive correspondence of More, and in only one early biography, is Elyot mentioned among More's friends. Thomas Stapleton, born the year More was beheaded, records in his *Life of More* (1588) simply that Elyot and More were friends, drawn together "in the pursuit of polite literature," and that Elyot's wife, Margaret, was a pupil in More's famous "school." Although their paths may have crossed rather frequently in affairs of state, it was no doubt chiefly an interest in literature and education that brought More and Elyot together. The degree of intimacy to which this interest may have led cannot be determined, although Elyot (adapting Cicero) makes a point of saying, in his chapter on friendship in Book II of *The Governor,* that "if similitude of study or learning be joined unto the said virtues, friendship much rather happeneth, and the mutual interview and conversation is much more pleasant, specially if the studies have in them any delectable affection or motion." Professor Lehmberg conjectures that, as frequent visitors to More's house between 1510 and 1530, Thomas and Margaret Elyot would have had occasion to meet the most famous scholars of the time, among them William Grocyn, John Colet, Thomas Linacre, William Lily, William Mountjoy, Hugh Latimer, Thomas Lupset, Reginald Pole, John Fisher, Cuthbert Tunstall, and perhaps even Erasmus. It may have been there also that the portrait drawings of Sir Thomas and Lady Elyot by Holbein, now at Windsor Castle, were made.

At any rate, the friendship with More and conversation with More's learned circle must have been extremely fruitful to the author of *The Governor* and other serious works, all of which touch upon to some extent the aims, the substance, the methods, and the benefits for the nation of a genuinely humanistic education. In these matters, if not in politics, Elyot and More were of one mind.

Elyot's first appointment came in 1510, when he was named Clerk to the Justices of Assize for the Western Circuit, a position he held until 1526 or 1527, a few years after the death of his father, one of the justices. In 1523 he was named Clerk of the King's Council by Wolsey, the Lord Chancellor; he retained this fairly important office until April 1530, some months after Wolsey's disgrace. In a letter to Cromwell written two years later, Elyot complains that during his six and a half years as clerk he served "without fee, without reward more than the ordinary; and that which more grieveth me, without thanks of the king, which I deserved . . . if his grace had been truly informed of me." After Wolsey's fall, a former patent for the clerkship having been found, Elyot was "discharged without any recompense, rewarded only with the order of knighthood, honorable and onerous, having much less to live on than before." He had apparently hoped through Wolsey's influence to be promoted to Master of the Rolls, but when that office fell vacant in 1534, it went, ironically enough, to Elyot's friend and patron Thomas Cromwell.

It was probably through Cromwell that Elyot came to the attention of Wolsey. Elyot's relations with Cromwell—a man described by one historian as "swift, ruthless, accurate, corrupt, a master of detail and inaccessible to sentiment"[4]—are (perhaps unfortunately) better documented than his relations with the two other great political leaders of Henry VIII's reign. Elyot apparently met Cromwell as early as 1519, when the latter was studying law in London. As with More, the basis for Elyot's friendship with Cromwell seems to have been a mutual interest in literature, although after Cromwell began his spectacular ascent to power, around 1530, Elyot was placed more and more in the position of suitor for Cromwell's favors. In various extant letters to Cromwell written between 1528 and 1536, Elyot signs himself, successively, "Your loving companion," "By him that loveth you," "Your poorest friend," "Yours to my little power," "Yours with true affection," "Yours unfeignedly," and "Yours most bounden." Such terms, and the tone of the letters themselves, do indicate a certain intimacy; the tone is also respectful, complaining, and frequently begging, as Elyot, ill paid and out of pocket for his various services to the king, requests Cromwell's assistance for financial compensation—some of the suppressed monastery lands or a pension—or for more lucrative office. In the mid-1530's, at the very height of the divorce crisis, Elyot seems to have come under suspicion of having papist sympathies (about which more will be said). In two letters to Cromwell written at that time he stoutly affirms his allegiance to the king's religious views; the second of these letters, written probably in 1537, contains a statement that, judged abstractly, may bring some discredit to Elyot's character: "I therefore beseech your good lordship now to lay apart the remembrance of the amity between me and Sir Thomas More, which was but

[4] H. A. L. Fisher, *The History of England from the Accession of Henry VII to the Death of Henry VIII (1485–1547)* (London: Longmans, Green, 1928), p. 295.

usque ad aras,[5] as is the proverb, considering that I was never so much addict unto him as I was unto truth and fidelity toward my sovereign lord."

From a safe vantage-point in the twentieth century, one can only say that Elyot's denial of friendship with the martyred More, however ignoble in principle, was necessary if Elyot was to save his own neck during the terrible latter half of the 1530's. The case also illustrates in a small way the often alleged ruthlessness of the king's minister, Cromwell, Elyot's supposed friend of long standing. There is some irony to be savored in the fact that Elyot, who aspired to high rank but never attained it, outlived his mighty friend-patron by six years, and died peacefully.

Elyot's principal residence until 1530 was at Long Combe, near Oxford. From 1530 to the end of his life he resided mostly at Carlton, in Cambridgeshire. Between 1515 and 1529 he served intermittently as justice of the peace for Oxfordshire and Wiltshire; in 1527 and 1529 he was sheriff of Oxfordshire and Berkshire; and in 1532–33 sheriff (reluctantly) of Cambridgeshire and Huntingdonshire. At Carlton, free from any major responsibility in English government for the first time in nearly twenty years, he wrote the first and most important of his works, *The Book Named the Governor,* which he dedicated to Henry VIII.

Professor Lehmberg thinks that at the instigation of Cromwell Elyot wrote *The Governor,* with its glorification of monarchy, partly as propaganda for the king's cause in the divorce issue and partly to ingratiate himself with Henry, with whom he may have lost favor because of his association with Wolsey. If that was his aim, he was successful, for in September 1531 he was appointed

---

[5] Literally, "as far as the altar."

ambassador to the court of the Holy Roman Emperor, Charles V.

Elyot's instructions from the king, set forth in detail and amounting to an argument, complete with possible refutations, were "to fish out and know in what opinion the emperor is of us" in the divorce matter. The new ambassador left for the emperor's court in October, and was replaced a few months later, in January 1532, by Thomas Cranmer. He may have been recalled at his own request —in a letter to Cromwell he complains of having amassed a large debt in carrying out his mission—or he may have been relieved for failing in his mission. He himself, at any rate, as he told the Duke of Norfolk, thought he had impressed the emperor: "in my replications [replies] I have seen him change countenance, which, as they know that have been with him, is no little thing." Awaiting his opportunity, and "using such a prince with silken words," Elyot "attained with him such familiarity in communication that he used with me more abundance of words than (as some of his Council confessed) any ambassador before me had found in him."

Before returning to England, Elyot visited various cities of the empire, among them Nuremberg, which he described to Norfolk as "the most proper town and best ordered public weal that ever I beheld." In Nuremberg he attended one of the churches, and, finding the reformed service strange, left before communion, "which caused all the people in the church to wonder at us, as if we had been greater heretics than they." After leaving Ratisbon, probably in April, he spent about a month in the Low Countries in an attempt to apprehend the heretic William Tyndale and bring him back to England. In this mission he had no success.

After his return to England, in June, he communicated

with the emperor's ambassador to England, Eustace
Chapuys, and with another agent of the emperor. Chapuys continued to cultivate Elyot, judging him sympathetic to Queen Catherine's cause, as he may well have
been. In a dispatch to the emperor written in 1534,
Chapuys names Elyot among the English gentlemen who
could be counted on to support a Spanish-led conspiracy
against the heretic Henry. Chapuys is not a very reliable
witness, but his remarks, together with some later charges
against Elyot, suggest that Elyot was playing a dangerous
game. It is perhaps not surprising that he fell in the
king's favor, as he complains in a letter of 1532 to Cromwell. Not only had he gone into great debt in the king's
service, but "I perceive the king's opinion minished
toward me by that, that I perceive other men advanced
openly to the place of counselors which neither in the
importance of service, neither in charges, have served
the king as I have done, and I, being omitted, had in less
estimation than I was in when I served the king first in
his Council." He protests that he speaks thus "not for
any ambition, but that only I desire that my true heart
should not cause me to live both in poverty and out of
estimation, for God judge my soul as I desire more to
live out of debt and in quiet study than to have as much
as a king may give me."

Elyot's complaints about the king's ingratitude, and
his judgment of the situation at court, may have found
their way into his next two or three publications. *Pasquil
the Plain* (1533) is a pasquinade or squib in dialogue
form attacking flattery in counselors. Pasquil, the plain
speaker or railer, is spokesman for Elyot himself; he
roundly criticizes both Gnatho for encouraging his master in wrongdoing and Harpocrates for giving his silent
approbation to the same wrongdoing. There are several

topical hints and references in the work, the most interesting being Pasquil's declaration that if people had listened to him instead of dismissing him as a babbler, "Germany should not have kicked against her mother; emperors and princes should not have been in perpetual discord and often times in peril; prelates have been laughed at, as dissardes [fools]; saints blasphemed, and miracles reproved for jugglings [impostures]; laws and statutes contemned, and officers little regarded."[6]

The *Doctrinal of Princes* (1533), a translation of Isocrates' oration *To Nicocles,* besides being Elyot's effort "to assay if our English tongue might receive the quick and proper sentences pronounced by the Greeks," could be considered a prince's mirror for his willful royal master. The work contains much sober advice of a gnomic kind on how to rule wisely, as for example:

Reward thy familiar counselors with principal dignities, and to them whom thou knowest benevolent and trusty, give perpetual and stable promotions.

Think that the best and most sure guard of thy person be friends virtuous and honest, loving and benevolent subjects, and thine own will stable and circumspect; for by those things, authority is obtained and longest preserved.

[This perhaps with More in mind especially] Take away fear from thy subjects, and be not terrible to them that have not offended. . . .

Think not them to be loyal or faithful that do praise all thing that thou doest, but them that do blame the thing wherein thou errest.

[6] Sir Thomas Elyot, *Four Political Treatises: "The Doctrinal of Princes" (1533), "Pasquil the Playne" (1533), "The Banquette of Sapience" (1534), "The Image of Governance" (1541),* with an introduction by Lillian Gottesman (Gainesville, Fla.: Scholars' Facsimiles and Reprints, 1967), p. 58.

Give to wise men liberty to speak to thee freely. . . .

Discern crafty flatterers from them that do serve thee with true heart and benevolence, lest the evil men receive more profit by thee than they that be honest and virtuous.[7]

In a more ambitious work of the same year, the Platonic dialogue *Of the Knowledge Which Maketh a Wise Man,* Elyot is at pains in the preface to deny, in the face of backbiters, that in any of his writings he aimed his criticisms at particular persons. He is grateful to Henry for having received his *Governor* "benignly," and for having approved his purpose in that work of augmenting the English language by introducing new words, which some readers found strange. Further, the king was not personally offended by even the sharper passages in the book; on the contrary, as it was reported to Elyot, "his grace not only took it in the better part, but also with princely words full of majesty commended my diligence, simplicity, and courage in that I spared none estate in the rebuking of vice." The king "perfectly knew that no writer ought to be blamed which writeth neither for hope of temporal reward nor for any private disdain or malice, but only of fervent zeal toward good occupation and virtue. Perdie[8] man is not yet so conformed in grace that he cannot do sin. And I suppose no prince thinketh himself to be exempt from mortality. And for as much as he shall have more occasions to fall, he ought to have the more friends or the more instruction to warn him."[9]

Elyot must have had some anxious moments. Never-

---

[7] *Ibid.,* pp. 16–21.

[8] Literally, "By God!" but often with the milder meaning of "verily."

[9] Sir Thomas Elyot, *Of the Knowledge Which Maketh a Wise Man,* edited by Edwin Johnston Howard (Oxford, O.: Anchor Press, 1946), pp. 4–9.

theless he went forward with his Platonic dialogue, which is also about the counseling of kings. Once when the philosopher Plato was serving Dionysius of Syracuse as counselor, he declared bluntly to that ruler that an action of his smacked of tyranny. Thereupon Dionysius grew furious and would have had Plato put to death if Plato had not fortunately escaped the city. The question of the dialogue, in which Plato and the philosopher Aristippus are speakers, is whether or not Plato was "wise" in speaking so plainly to Dionysius and thereby endangering his life. The conclusion of the long argument, which uses with intermittent skill the ideas of Plato's own dialogues, is that Plato did the wise thing, since the knowledge that is wisdom is goodness or right action.

These three works on counsel, published within a few months of each other, were probably inspired primarily by Elyot's humanistic creed—which compelled him to use his talents to the benefit of his country and its ruler, never more in need of wise counsel—and secondarily by the desire to convince Henry that Elyot should be appointed in person to his Council. One wishes to believe also, if only for sentimental reasons, that these and later works represented Elyot's attempt to help his friend More, who had resigned the chancellorship in May 1532 —in a real sense a wise counselor had been dismissed by a tyrant who could not stomach his honesty—and who was awaiting the inevitable imprisonment that was to come two years later. Although this is only a conjecture, it does have some support from the nature of the works themselves, from details within the works, and from external circumstances.[10]

[10] See the argument in my book, *Sir Thomas Elyot and Renaissance Humanism* (Lincoln: University of Nebraska Press, 1964), pp. 96–109. I now feel that I somewhat overstated the case there.

There seems to have been a fairly widespread belief that Elyot favored "superstition" and the papacy. Though he himself is caustic in his published writings about monks, friars, and the rest of the unpopular side of the Roman Church, Chapuys considered him sympathetic to Catherine's cause, and his friendship with More got him in trouble after More's downfall. In April 1533 Elyot wrote to John Hackett, the English ambassador to the Low Countries: "I would that I had some comfortable news to send you out of these parts, but the world is all otherwise. I beseech our lord amend it. We have hanging over us a great cloud, which is likely to be a great storm when it falleth." As to his own stand, Elyot says that he is "determined to live and die" in the true faith, and, in spite of disappointments in his professional life, to support the king.

In May of the same year Anne Boleyn was publicly acknowledged as queen, and Elyot was among the knights and gentlemen in attendance at her coronation. Chapuys was probably in error when, in an earlier dispatch (1531), he described Elyot as being in the service of Anne ("the Lady"); it is much more likely that he was a partisan of Catherine, although he could have been playing a double game. Professor Lehmberg thinks that Elyot's little work, *A Defense of Good Women* (1540), is a tribute to Catherine's courage and goodness; it may be, although the book is dedicated to Henry's third wife, Anne of Cleves! We are dealing with a complicated period.

By December 1534 Elyot was on the defensive about his religion. In a letter to Cromwell, he admits to having in his possession some books which had been declared seditious—books supporting the pope's authority and "divers other works"—though he has seen through their errors. He offers to search his houses for these books and either submit them to Cromwell or destroy them. As for his own fidelity, "Perchance natural simplicity not discreetly ordered might cause men to suspect I favored hypocrisy, superstition, and vanity. Notwithstanding, if ye might see my thoughts as God doth, ye should find a reformer of those things and not a favorer, if I might that I would."

Two years later a certain John Parkyns, whom G. R. Elton calls the "Fool of Oxford," made wild and incoherent charges about Elyot's consorting with Oxfordshire abbots and others suspected of Roman leanings. The charges were officially dismissed as baseless, and Parkyns was punished for false accusation. Nevertheless, the suspicion was there, and must have cost Elyot some uneasy moments. The letter to Cromwell in which Elyot rejects More probably dates from this time. After assuring Cromwell once again of his loyalty, Elyot proceeds: "I perceive that ye suspect that I savor not truly holy scripture. I would God that the king and you might see the most secret thoughts of my heart. Surely ye should then perceive that, the order of charity saved, I have in as much detestation as any man living all vain superstitions, superfluous ceremonies, slanderous jugglings, counterfeit miracles, arrogant usurpations of men called spiritual and masking religious, and all other abusions of Christ's holy doctrine and laws. And as much I enjoy at the king's godly proceeding to the due reformation of the said enormities as any his grace's poor subject living." It is sad to see Elyot cringing in this fashion, but to such abasement were Englishmen—all but the handful of martyrs—driven by the madness of the time.

To conclude this account of Elyot's religious views, it is clear that, whatever his real attitude toward Rome, he detested Lutheranism. In his last work, *A Preservative*

Against Death (1545), he came out strongly against pre-destination, justification by faith alone, and personal interpretation of Scripture; against these he asserted the freedom of the will and general grace to sinners. Taken as a whole, his religious position, while it may appear from the evidence to be rather ambiguous, was probably not untypical of that held by most Englishmen of his class. It is summarized by Professor Lehmberg as follows:

> Had the path of Erasmian reform still been open Elyot would no doubt have chosen it. He would not follow More to the block over the question of the supremacy; besides wanting to preserve his neck intact he probably believed conscientiously that the King was more likely to reform abuses than the Pope. So far, but no farther: Elyot never suggested, even in his most servile letter, that he would willingly see the King tamper with the traditional beliefs and ceremonies. He hoped for superficial purification without fundamental change.[11]

The latter years of Elyot's life seem to have been relatively uneventful. We hear of his being a member of the Parliaments of 1539 and 1542, probably for the borough of Cambridge; he was among the knights and squires appointed to receive Anne of Cleves in 1540; and he served on various commissions between 1540 and 1544. No doubt he devoted much of his time during this period to managing his by then considerable estates and to study and writing, in particular the Latin-English *Dictionary*, which was first printed in 1538 and republished (as *Bibliotheca Eliotae*) in an enlarged edition in 1542 and 1545. He died some ten months before the king whom he had served so many years, on March 26, 1546, at Carlton in Cambridgeshire, and was buried there in the parish church.

[11] *Sir Thomas Elyot: Tudor Humanist,* pp. 150–151.

In addition to the works already mentioned, Elyot is author of *The Banquet of Sapience* (c. 1534), a collection of the sayings of wise men; *The Castle of Health* (c. 1536), a popular book of medical remedies, the product in part of his study during youth with a "worshipful physician," thought to be Linacre; and *The Image of Governance* (1541), a prince's mirror in the form of a largely fictitious life of the emperor Alexander Severus. He also translated, besides the oration of Isocrates referred to earlier, Pico della Mirandola's *The Rules of a Christian Life* (1534), St. Cyprian's *A Sweet and Devout Sermon . . . of the Mortality of Man* (1534), and Plutarch's *The Education or Bringing Up of Children* (1533?), the last for the benefit of the two small sons of his sister Margery Puttenham, one of whom later wrote the celebrated *Art of English Poesy* (1589).

Looking at Elyot's writings as a whole, one can see that they are all serious and didactic and that within this range they reveal a wide variety of concerns: politics, law, moral philosophy, religion, education, history, poetry, language, lexicography, and medicine. As a Christian humanist par excellence, Elyot was bent on sharing with others less informed the fruits of his study, on bringing enlightenment to an England which had lagged behind in the cultural revolution of the Renaissance—and all this to the greater glory of God, author of all knowledge and wisdom. Education is for him the key to understanding, to virtue, progress, and power; and since the highest reaches of learning had been attained by the ancients, Elyot, like the other humanists, stresses the primacy in the educational process of a knowledge of classical literature. For him, the ideal man or gentleman is above all virtuous; he is also learned, articulate, and public-spirited—a kind of combination of Cicero's orator,

Castiglione's courtier, Erasmus' Christian prince, and English knight.

We come now to an examination of Elyot's most ambitious and durable work, *The Book Named the Governor,* which stands alongside More's *Utopia* and Roger Ascham's *The Schoolmaster* as a splendid example of Tudor humanist thought expressed in literary prose. Though *The Governor* is primarily a book of education, it is set in a political frame, and the emphasis throughout is placed on education for government service. Thus the work opens with three chapters on government—the true public weal, to the maintenance of which in prosperity the ideal education is designed, requires a monarch, lesser magistrates or governors, and distinct social classes—and closes with two chapters on the political art of counseling, to the perfection of which the governor's entire education has been directed. The kind of education described in *The Governor* is frankly aristocratic. It is intended for the sons of noblemen and gentlemen, it stresses good letters (although not to the neglect of experience), and it aims at perpetuating a society dominated and led by an aristocracy whose support is provided, as their due, by the lower social orders. No doubt *The Governor* was in part written as Henrician-Cromwellian propaganda; and it opposes, deliberately or not, the ideal state described in More's *Utopia,* with its various democratic institutions, its elected monarch, and its classless society.

Some qualifications of these remarks need to be added, however: if Elyot's bias is aristocratic, at the same time he allows for advancement of the poor and obscure man through talent, as developed by learning. He himself, like his great patrons Wolsey and Cromwell, is an example of the man of modest background promoted to office by a shrewd king who valued and rewarded learning.

And now to Elyot's plan of education for the nobleman's child. He would have him educated at home, by a tutor or master, from age five or so to twenty-one (Elyot is vague about time), in the *encyclopedia* or circle of arts and sciences, after which the student would presumably go on to the university or to a school of law. From the beginning, the emphasis, in good humanist fashion, is placed on the building of the child's character through the tutor's selection and interpretation of authors and works to be read, but above all through the good example set by the tutor himself. To the modern reader, Elyot's worries (in Chapters 4 and 6) about the infant's and young child's moral environment may seem exaggerated and even amusing, but he is merely repeating standard doctrine of the time as set down by Erasmus, Colet, and other humanist educators.

In this strictly moral atmosphere, then, the child at the tender age of five, when our century's children are playing "constructively" with toys, is taught to draw the letters of the alphabet, to speak Latin, and to understand the rudiments of grammar. All this is, of course, preparation for more difficult study, which begins when the child is seven. Since most of the discussion and reading is to be done in Latin (some of it in Greek), the child must necessarily be introduced early and easily to the Latin tongue. Right from the start Elyot emphasizes three things which the Renaissance learned from the wise Roman, Quintilian: that study should be made pleasant for the child, that the schoolmaster should avoid cruelty, and that he should early discover the child's character and also his bent or aptitude, and foster those impulses which accord with virtue. One of the leisure occupations of the child, for example, is painting and carving; Elyot asks that noblemen overcome their distaste for this manual skill and encourage their sons, if they show interest and talent, to practice it. Because of the aristocratic snobbery toward performing arts, England has lost "many good wits," and "in the said arts Englishmen be inferiors to all other people, and be constrained, if we will have anything well painted, carved, or embroidered, to abandon our own countrymen and resort unto strangers" (Chapter 14).

Another recreation for the child is music (Chapter 7). In recommending the visual arts and music, Elyot is torn between his own obvious love for these things on the one hand, and on the other his sober humanist detestation of idleness or wantonness and—under the influence of Castiglione, probably—his sense of gentlemanly decorum: It simply would not do for a gentle or noble person to soil himself overmuch in making works of art or to perform music in public or abandon himself to the sensuous pleasures of these enterprises. He must get on steadily with the serious business of learning how to govern a public weal. Yet there are pragmatic benefits: a knowledge and practice of painting will give the future governor a good eye for military terrain, for the condition of his dominions, and for supervising building on his estates; it will also sharpen his imagination and memory and even his moral zeal. Likewise music can be shown, on the authority of Plato and Aristotle, to illustrate the necessary harmony in a public weal.

Despite these hesitations, Elyot does stick to his principle that learning for the young child should be delightful as well as serious. Thus at age seven the child begins study (Chapter 10) of Aesop's *Fables,* which "is a much pleasant lesson and also profitable." Next he may take up some "quick and merry dialogues" of Lucian—a favorite author of the early humanists—or the comedies of Aristophanes. This might seem to us like pretty strong stuff for seven- or eight-year-olds, but Elyot would have the master make a selection from these authors, omitting what is ribald or excessively scornful. (Later in *The Governor*, Elyot defends all poets as worthy to be read by a mature student.) The divine Homer comes next, "from whom, as from a fountain, proceeded all eloquence and learning." Elyot read Homer and Virgil as Sidney and Spenser did, allegorically: from the *Iliad*, for example, a man can gather "courage and strength against his enemies, wisdom and eloquence for consultations and persuasions to his people and army." No one author has such wide appeal as Virgil: children take delight ("as I know by mine own experience") in the pastoral charm of the *Eclogues*, the beauty of nature, the practical husbandry, and the astronomy of the *Georgics*, and the world of absorbing activities in the *Aeneid*. Ovid and Horace, Silius Italicus, Lucan, and Hesiod round out the reading of the poets, which the child continues until thirteen or fourteen, at which time "childhood declineth, and reason waxeth ripe, and deprehendeth [comprehends] things with a more constant judgment." In other words, he is now ready for more "serious" subjects. The desired effect of reading poetry, it seems, is to "inflame" the child to have experience in those things which poets commend. Tragedies, which teach men to "execrate and abhor the intolerable life of tyrants" (as Sidney was to say later), and the right reading of "poets lascivious" are reserved for the student's maturity, when "reason in him is confirmed with serious learning and long experience."

Elyot's concept of poetry as pleasing instruction for

childish minds is, from a modern standpoint, not exactly flattering to that high art, but it would not have offended Francis Bacon. And Elyot takes such wholehearted personal delight in Homer, Virgil, and the others that we can forgive him his no doubt unintended slight.

Elyot's attitude toward the study of grammar, logic, and rhetoric (Chapters 10, 11, 13), those staples of the Renaissance curriculum, is very enlightened. Like Milton some hundred years later, Elyot would have the young child learn only so much of the rules of grammar as is necessary to an understanding of the poets. If grammar is "made too long or exquisite to the learner," it dampens his spirit, and causes him to dislike literature. Logic (Milton would agree to this, too) is not undertaken until the child is fifteen, along with rhetoric, and in connection with the study of oratory. Mere eloquence—words without matter—is scorned by Elyot, as it was by Erasmus and Bacon. One cause of the decay of learning, Elyot complains (in Chapter 13), is the negligence of parents, who, as soon as their sons have mastered grammar, Latin eloquence, and the making of Latin verses—at age fourteen—put a stop to their liberal education, and either allow them to live in idleness or put them to service. These victims of an incomplete education and of a false sense of cultural values (loosely, and somewhat unfairly, termed Ciceronianism by the Renaissance), after they have grown to manhood, not only forget their skill in speaking but hold all learning in contempt.

This is not to say that Elyot, or his compeers, rejected eloquence. On the contrary, they held it in highest esteem, as that ability which finally exalted man over the animals, gave him his dignity. What Erasmus and Elyot and Bacon were criticizing was the abuse of this art, or, more precisely, the rather widespread practice of making eloquence an end in itself, without regard to content or what was said. Cicero himself remains the ideal: the man of supreme eloquence who used his gift to the increase of virtue and to the political health of his country.

Following the study of poetry, then, the child, at age fifteen, takes up the study of oratory, with its constituent subjects, logic and rhetoric (Chapter 11). The perfect models, needless to say, are the great classical orators, Isocrates, Demosthenes, and Cicero. The "utility" that a nobleman will gain from reading them is that he will be able to reason well in council and speak effectively "in a great audience, or to strange ambassadors of great princes." Note that once again, the emphasis is on what is practical and useful. Next the student is introduced to geography and cosmography, the science which describes and maps the general features of the universe, both the heavens and the earth. Both of these subjects, we are assured, offer the desired pleasure and "commodity."

The youth is now ready for that favorite subject of the Renaissance, history. "Next to the works of ethical philosophers," it has been said, "and the sayings of the wise culled from experience, the 'Prince,' the 'Governor,' or the 'Gentleman' was to be formed by the study of history. It would be easy to fill a volume with the praise of history from the prefaces of scholars in the Renaissance."[12] Elyot follows North, the authors of *A Mirror for Magistrates,* and other Renaissance writers in favoring the Plutarchan or biographical kind of history, which taught the past through its great men, providing examples of conduct for the modern statesman to emulate

[12] Henry Burrowes Lathrop, *Translations from the Classics into English from Caxton to Chapman, 1477–1620,* University of Wisconsin Studies in Language and Literature Number 35 (Madison: University of Wisconsin, 1933), pp. 79–80.

or shun. One also found in history patterns of the rise
and fall of states, and drew from them object lessons for
contemporary politics. (Now and then in his writings
Elyot makes veiled reference to sixteenth-century England through illustrations from Greek and especially
Roman history, and occasionally from Italian and English.)

The value of studying history is that it provides a kind
of experience; and experience, whether actual or vicari-
ous, is essential to a complete education, since it tempers
and refines the knowledge or theory gained from books.
This is basic Renaissance educational doctrine. Its importance to Elyot is shown in the fact that, after stating
it in Book I of *The Governor,* he reasserts it at the very
end of that work, in Chapter 25 of Book III: "Of Experience Which Have Preceded Our Time, with a Defense of Histories," and in the succeeding chapter: "The
Experience or Practice Necessary in the Person of a Governor of a Public Weal." After the governor has investi-
gated, examined, and tried by experience the "griefs or
diseases which of Aristotle be called the decays of the
public weal," then comes the time of consultation,
whereby "is provided the remedies most necessary for
the healing of the said griefs or reparation of decays"
(Book III, Chapter 28). Consultation and the giving of
counsel are, in Elyot's scheme, the end product or goal
of a total education, which provides the kind of wisdom
compounded of learning and experience.

In part, this stress on experience is defensive: if Elyot
were to claim too much for learning alone, he would be
loudly rebuked by those all too numerous English governors of noble blood who not only had little learning
but who were proud of the fact. Elyot and the other humanist educators had to fight the traditional aristocratic

prejudice against learning as a thing suited to clerks, the fit occupations for gentlemen being warfare, hunting, hawking, and management of estates. Roger Ascham refuses to make Elyot's concessions: "Surely," he writes, "long experience doth profit much, but most, and almost only, to him (if we mean honest affairs) that is diligently before instructed with precepts of well-doing. . . . Learning teacheth more in one year than experience in twenty, and learning teacheth safely, when experience maketh more miserable than wise."[13] Quotation and paraphrase from historians and biographers abound in *The Governor* and in Elyot's other writings, almost as if to strengthen the author's point about the importance of history as experience and example, though more obviously, to enliven his discourse with anecdote. Plutarch, Livy, Tacitus, and the *Historia Augusta* are favorite authorities, and Alexander the Great, Julius Caesar, and the virtuous Roman emperors are favorite heroes. Elyot's admiration of history is summed up in a sentence in Book II (Chapter 1): "More semblable [similar] examples shall hereof be found by them which purposely do read histories, whom of all other I most desire to be princes and governors."

Following the study of history, when the future governor is seventeen, "to the intent his courage [spirit] be bridled with reason," the master shall read to him some works of moral philosophy (Chapter 11), notably the dialogues of Plato, Aristotle's *Nicomachaean Ethics,* Cicero's *De officiis,* and the "historical parts" of the Bible (the New Testament, as William Tyndale learned to his destruction, was sacred ground, for the church only to

---

[13] Roger Ascham, *The Schoolmaster (1570),* edited by Lawrence V. Ryan, Folger Documents of Tudor and Stuart Civilization (Ithaca: Cornell University Press, 1967), p. 50.

touch). Moral philosophy is the crown of Elyot's curriculum, and he waxes eloquent over the benefits of this study. Poetry and history, with their primary appeal to the heart and the imagination, have inflamed the child's "courage," made him aspire to do great and good deeds; moral philosophy will temper that noble excitement with reason, now that he has become mature and can comprehend principles of right action.

This concludes the formal course of study proposed in *The Governor*. Although, oddly enough, no mention is made of mathematics, one assumes that that subject would to some extent enter into the study of cosmography, and perhaps of philosophy; otherwise, the curriculum seems basic and sound, and well designed to train governors of the public weal, who are to be, above all, good men, and men of understanding. Elyot does insist that the student complete the full course: in a digression (Chapters 12, 13) he complains that learning has decayed in his time and country, the reasons being the noblemen's contempt for it, the stinginess of parents (compare Robert Burton's glorious harangue), who pay their falconer or cook more than their children's schoolmaster and thus get an ignorant schoolmaster, and parents' shortsightedness in pulling their sons out of school as soon as they have learned a smattering of Latin. In a later chapter (14) Elyot complains further that young men are sent to law school before they have been fully educated in the liberal arts. Elyot would have them "retained in the right study of very philosophy until they passed the age of twenty-one years, and then set to the laws of this realm." Only then, and after the laws themselves have been translated out of barbarous law French "into pure Latin or douce French," will England have sound laws and worthy lawyers and counselors.

Except for an interesting defense of poetry (Chapter 13)—perhaps the first in English, and anticipating many of Sidney's arguments—the remainder of Book I of *The Governor* describes the physical exercises in which the future governor should engage. True to the humanist ideal of education of the whole man, and indulging an Englishman's love of sports, Elyot recommends the toughening of the body, in preparation for the rigors of governing and more particularly of military combat, through such exercises as wrestling, running, swimming, exercising with the sword and battle axe, hunting, hawking, and dancing. The "most honorable" exercise, "and that beseemeth the estate of every noble person, is to ride surely and clean on a great horse and a rough." In every instance, a nobleman should not compete with his social inferiors (Castiglione would agree to this), and rough sports that lead to violence and anger, like football, are to be eschewed. Another advantage of exercise is that it prevents idleness, "the nurse of vices," a horrible example of which is playing at dice. Elyot devotes a whole chapter (27) to shooting with the long bow, anticipating Ascham's *Toxophilus* (1545) in calling it "principal of all other exercises." Since in the past this weapon had brought England great military victories, Elyot, like Ascham, laments its decline, and invokes enforcement of the laws requiring Englishmen to train with it.

The chapters on dancing (19 to 25) make a fascinating little treatise on that subject, borrowing from Plato, Aristotle, Lucian, and the custom, probably medieval in origin, of allegorizing games and exercises: in hunting, for example, "may be an imitation of battle," and Elyot mentions with approval a popular book of the time, William Caxton's translation from the French of *The Game and Play of the Chess* (1476, 1483), which "moralizes" that game. After first allaying the church-inspired suspicions of dancing, Elyot recalls its esteem in antiquity and then proceeds to show, rather quaintly, how the dancing together of a man and a woman, through the various steps, illustrates the virtue prudence and its components, thus proving both the pleasantness and the edifying effects of this exercise.

Books II and III of *The Governor* are, respectively, a book of courtesy or manners and a treatise of ethical philosophy, both books owing much to Plato, Aristotle, and Cicero, and each having, as a secondary aim, augmenting of the English language through definition and the introduction of new terms. The various virtues or manners discussed in Book II, taken together, make up an extra cardinal virtue, as it were—"true nobility," which Elyot defines as "only the praise and surname of virtue," but adding, "the longer it continueth in a name or lineage, the more is nobility extolled and marvelled at" (Book II, Chapter 4). The counsel offered in Book II to the governor, who has by this time received his first appointment, consists mostly of antidotes to pride and vainglory. Book III treats in detail the cardinal virtues justice, fortitude, temperance, and sapience or wisdom (prudence having already been analyzed in Book I in the chapters on dancing).

This, then, is Sir Thomas Elyot's *The Book Named the Governor,* a work of education which combined the practical and the ideal, the traditional and the innovative, common sense and moral conviction. In its entirety, as we see, *The Governor* is not narrowly or technically confined to education but reaches beyond it into the realm of philosophy. It is very much a Renaissance book, with its continuing emphasis on the inculcation of goodness in the citizen and on training for usefulness in society. Elyot was seeking to mold the complete English gentleman—virtuous, learned, courteous, responsible, and efficient—and through him, a flourishing English society (the *Republic* of Plato is never far from his thoughts). The spirit of Christian humanism which pervades the whole work is beautifully expressed in the final paragraph:

Now all ye readers that desire to have your children to be governors, or in any other authority in the public weal of your country, if ye bring them up and instruct them in such form as in this book is declared, they shall then seem to all men worthy to be in authority, honor, and noblesse, and all that is under their governance shall prosper and come to perfection. And as a precious stone in a rich ouche [setting] they shall be beholden and wondered at, and after the death of their body their souls for their endeavor shall be incomprehensibly rewarded of the giver of wisdom, to whom only be eternal glory. Amen.

It is not an exaggeration to say that *The Governor* set the pattern for the right education of an English gentleman and public servant. Elyot's work is a worthy successor to the writings of the Italian humanists and Erasmus, and a worthy predecessor to Ascham's *Schoolmaster*, Henry Peacham's *Complete Gentleman*, and Milton's *Of Education*. It was read profitably by Spenser, Shakespeare, Jonson, Bacon, and, in our time, T. S. Eliot. It is truly a classic in education.

THE PROEM

The Proem of Thomas Elyot, Knight,
unto the Most Noble and Victorious Prince,
King Henry the Eighth, King of England and France, Defender of
the True Faith, and Lord
of Ireland

I late considering (most excellent prince and mine only
redoubted sovereign lord) my duty that I owe to my
natural country, with my faith also of allegiance and
oath, wherewith I am double bounden unto your majesty; moreover, the account that I have to render for
that one little talent delivered to me, to employ (as I
suppose) to the increase of virtue—I am (as God judge
me) violently stirred to divulgate or set forth some part
of my study, trusting thereby to acquit me of my duties
to God, your highness, and this my country. Wherefore
taking comfort and boldness partly of your grace's most
benevolent inclination toward the universal weal of your
subjects, partly inflamed with zeal, I have now enterprised to describe in our vulgar tongue the form of a
just public weal: which matter I have gathered as well
of the sayings of most noble authors (Greeks and Latins)
as by mine own experience, I being continually trained
in some daily affairs of the public weal of this your most

noble realm almost from my childhood. Which attempt
is not of presumption to teach any person, I myself having most need of teaching; but only to the intent that
men which will be studious about the weal public may
find the thing thereto expedient compendiously written.
And for as much as this present book treateth of the
education of them that hereafter may be deemed worthy
to be governors of the public weal under your highness
(which Plato affirmeth to be the first and chief part of
a public weal, Solomon saying also, where governors be
not, the people shall fall into ruin), I therefore have
named it *The Governor.* I do now dedicate it unto your
highness as the first fruits of my study, verily trusting
that your most excellent wisdom will therein esteem my
loyal heart and diligent endeavor, by the example of
Artaxerxes the noble king of Persia, who rejected not
the poor husbandman which offered to him his homely
hands full of clean water, but most graciously received
it with thanks, esteeming the present not after the value,
but rather to the will of the giver. Semblably[1] King
Alexander retained with him the poet Cherilus honorably, for writing his history, although that the poet was
but of a small estimation; which that prince did, not
for lack of judgment, he being of excellent learning as
disciple to Aristotle, but to the intent that his liberality
employed on Cherilus should animate or give courage
to others much better learned, to contend with him in a
semblable enterprise. And if, most virtuous prince, I
may perceive your highness to be herewith pleased, I
shall soon after (God giving me quietness) present your
grace with the residue of my study and labors. Wherein
your highness shall well perceive that I nothing esteem
so much in this world as your royal estate (my most dear
sovereign lord) and the public weal of my country, pro-

testing unto your excellent majesty that where I commend
herein any one virtue or dispraise any one vice, I mean the
general description of the one and the other without any
other particular meaning to the reproach of any one person; to the which protestation I am now driven through
the malignity of this present time, all disposed to mali-
cious detraction. Wherefore I most humbly beseech your
highness to deign to be patron and defender of this
little work against the assaults of malign interpreters, which fail not to rent[2] and deface the
renown of writers, they themselves being
in nothing to the public weal profitable;
which is by no man sooner perceived
than by your highness, being
both in wisdom and very
nobility
equal
to the most excellent
princes, whom I beseech God ye
may surmount in long life and perfect felicity.
Amen.

[1] Similarly
[2] rend

The Table

THE SECOND BOOK

THE THIRD BOOK

THE FIRST BOOK

The Signification of a Public Weal, and Why It Is Called in Latin *Respublica*

A public weal is in sundry wise defined by philosophers; but knowing by experience that the often repetition of anything of grave or sad importance will be tedious to the readers of this work, who perchance for the more part have not been trained in learning containing semblable[1] matter, I have compiled one definition out of many, in as compendious form as my poor wit can devise, trusting that in those few words the true signification of a public weal shall evidently appear to them whom reason can satisfy.

A public weal is a body living, compact or made of sundry estates and degrees of men, which is disposed by the order of equity and governed by the rule and moderation of reason. In the Latin tongue it is called *respublica,* of the which the word *res* hath divers significations, and doth not only betoken that that is called a thing, which is distinct from a person, but also signifieth estate, condition, substance, and profit. In our vulgar, profit is called weal; and it is called a wealthy country wherein is all thing that is profitable; and he is a wealthy man that is rich in money and substance. Public (as Varro saith) is derived of people, which in Latin is called *populus.* Wherefore it seemeth that men have been long abused in

[1] similar

calling *rempublicam* a common weal. And they which
do suppose it so to be called for that, that everything
should be to all men in common, without discrepance of
any estate or condition, be thereto moved more by sensu-
ality than by any good reason or inclination to humanity.
And that shall soon appear unto them that will be satisfied either with authority or with natural order and example.

First, the proper and true signification of the words
public and common, which be borrowed of the Latin
tongue for the insufficiency of our own language, shall
sufficiently declare the blindness of them which have
hitherto holden and maintained the said opinions. As I
have said, public took his beginning of people, which in
Latin is *populus,* in which word is contained all the inhabitants of a realm or city, of what estate or condition
soever they be.

Plebs in English is called the commonalty, which signifieth only the multitude, wherein be contained the
base and vulgar inhabitants not advanced to any honor
or dignity; which is also used in our daily communication, for in the city of London and other cities, they that
be none aldermen or sheriffs be called commoners; and
in the country at a sessions or other assembly, if no
gentlemen be thereat, the saying is, that there was none
but the commonalty; which proveth in mine opinion
that *plebs* in Latin is in English commonalty, and *plebeii*
be commoners. And consequently there may appear like
diversity to be in English between a public weal and a
common weal as should be in Latin between *respublica*
and *resplebeia.* And after that signification, if there
should be a common weal, either the commoners only
must be wealthy, and the gentle and noble men needy
and miserable, or else, excluding gentility, all men must

be of one degree and sort, and a new name provided: for
as much as *plebs* in Latin and commoners in English be
words only made for the discrepance of degrees, whereof
proceedeth order, which in things as well natural as super-
natural hath ever had such a pre-eminence that thereby
the incomprehensible majesty of God, as it were by a
bright leme[2] of a torch or candle, is declared to the blind
inhabitants of this world. Moreover, take away order
from all things, what should then remain? Certes[3] nothing, finally, except some man would imagine eftsoons[4]
chaos, which of some is expound a confuse[d] mixture.
Also where there is any lack of order, needs must be
perpetual conflict. And in things subject to nature, nothing of himself only may be nourished; but when he hath
destroyed that wherewith he doth participate by the
order of his creation, he himself of necessity must then
perish, whereof ensueth universal dissolution.

But now to prove, by example of those things that be
within the compass of man's knowledge, of what estimation order is, not only among men, but also with God,
albeit his wisdom, bounty, and magnificence can be with
no tongue or pen sufficiently expressed. Hath not he set
degrees and estates in all his glorious works?

First, in his heavenly ministers, whom, as the church
affirmeth, he hath constituted to be in divers degrees,
called hierarchs. Also Christ saith by his evangelist that
in the house of his father (which is God) be many man-
sions. But to treat of that which by natural understanding may be comprehended, behold the four elements
whereof the body of man is compact, how they be set in
their places, called spheres, higher or lower, according to
the sovereignty of their natures. That is to say, the fire, as

[2] gleam   [3] Assuredly
[4] forthwith

the most pure element, having in it nothing that is corruptible, in his place is highest and above other elements. The air, which next to the fire is most pure in substance, is in the second sphere or place. The water, which is somewhat consolidate and approacheth to corruption, is next unto the earth. The earth, which is of substance gross and ponderous, is set of all elements most lowest.

Behold also the order that God hath put generally in all his creatures, beginning at the most inferior or base, and ascending upward. He made not only herbs to garnish the earth, but also trees of a more eminent stature than herbs, and yet in the one and the other be degrees of qualities, some pleasant to behold, some delicate or good in taste, other wholesome and medicinable, some commodious and necessary. Semblably in birds, beasts, and fishes, some be good for the sustenance of man, some bear things profitable to sundry uses, other be apt to occupation and labor; in divers is strength and fierceness only; in many is both strength and commodity; some other serve for pleasure; none of them hath all these qualities; few have the more part or many, specially beauty, strength, and profit. But where any is found that hath many of the said properties, he is more set by than all the other, and by that estimation the order of his place and degree evidently appeareth. So that every kind of trees, herbs, birds, beasts, and fishes, beside their diversity of forms, have (as who saith) a peculiar disposition appropered[5] unto them by God their creator. So that in everything is order; and without order may be nothing stable or permanent; and it may not be called order except it do contain in it degrees, high and base, according to the merit or estimation of the thing that is ordered.

Now to return to the estate of mankind, for whose use

[5] assigned

all the said creatures were ordained of God, and also excelleth them all by prerogative of knowledge and wisdom,
it seemeth that in him should be no less providence of
God declared than in the inferior creatures, but rather
with a more perfect order and disposition. And therefore it appeareth that God giveth not to every man like
gifts of grace, or of nature, but to some more, some less,
as it liketh his divine majesty. Ne[6] they be not in common (as fantastical fools would have all things), nor one
man hath not all virtues and good qualities. Notwithstanding, for as much as understanding is the most excellent gift that man can receive in his creation, whereby
he doth approach most nigh unto the similitude of God,
which understanding is the principal part of the soul, it
is therefore congruent, and according, that as one excelleth another in that influence, as thereby being next
to the similitude of his maker, so should the estate of his
person be advanced in degree, or place, where understanding may profit; which is also distributed into sundry
uses, faculties, and offices necessary for the living and
governance of mankind.

And like as the angels which be most fervent in contemplation be highest exalted in glory (after the opinion
of holy doctors), and also the fire, which is the most pure
of elements, and also doth clarify the other inferior elements, is deputed to the highest sphere or place, so in
this world, they which excel other in this influence of
understanding, and do employ it to the detaining of other
within the bounds of reason, and show them how to
provide for their necessary living—such ought to be set
in a more high place than the residue, where they may
see, and also be seen, that by the beams of their excellent
wit, showed through the glass of authority, other of

[6] Nor

inferior understanding may be directed to the way of
virtue and commodious living. And unto men of such
virtue by very equity apperteineth honor, as their just
reward and duty; which by other men's labors must also
be maintained, according to their merits: for as much as
the said persons excelling in knowledge, whereby other
be governed, be ministers for the only profit and commodity of them which have not equal understanding;
where they which do exercise artificial science, or cor-
poral labor, do not travail for their superiors only, but
also for their own necessity. So the husbandman feedeth
himself and the cloth maker; the cloth maker apparelleth
himself and the husband; they both succor other artificers; other artificers, them; they and other artificers, them
that be governors. But they that be governors (as I before said) nothing do acquire by the said influence of
knowledge for their own necessities, but do employ all
the powers of their wits and their diligence to the only
preservation of other their inferiors. Among which inferiors also behoveth to be a disposition and order according to reason; that is to say, that the slothful or idle
person do not participate with him that is industrious
and taketh pain, whereby the fruits of his labors should
be diminished; wherein should be none equality, but
thereof should proceed discourage, and finally dissolution for lack of provision.

Wherefore it can none otherwise stand with reason,
but that the estate of the person in pre-eminence of living should be esteemed with his understanding, labor,
and policy; whereunto must be added an augmentation
of honor and substance, which not only impresseth a
reverence, whereof proceedeth due obedience among
subjects, but also inflameth men naturally inclined to

idleness or sensual appetite to covet like fortune, and for that cause to dispose them to study or occupation.

Now to conclude my first assertion or argument: where all thing is common, there lacketh order; and where order lacketh, there all thing is odious and uncomely. And that have we in daily experience, for the pans and pots garnisheth well the kitchen, and yet should they be to the chamber none ornament. Also the beds, testers, and pillows beseemeth not the hall, no more than the carpets and cushions becometh the stable. Semblably the potter and tinker, only perfect in their craft, shall little do in the ministration of justice. A plowman or carter shall make but a feeble answer to an ambassador. Also a weaver or fuller[7] should be an unmeet captain of an army or in any other office of a governor. Wherefore, to conclude, it is only a public weal where, like as God hath disposed the said influence of understanding, is also appointed degrees and places according to the excellency thereof, and thereto also would be substance convenient and necessary for the ornament of the same; which also impresseth a reverence and due obedience to the vulgar people or commonalty; and without that it can be no more said that there is a public weal than it may be affirmed that a house without his proper and necessary ornaments is well and sufficiently furnished.

[7] one who treads or beats cloth for the purpose of cleansing and thickening it

2

That One Sovereign Governor Ought to Be in a Public Weal; and What Damage Hath Happened Where a Multitude Hath Had Equal Authority Without Any Sovereign

Like as to a castle or fortress sufficeth one owner or sovereign, and where any more be of like power and authority, seldom cometh the work to perfection; or being already made, where the one diligently overseeth, and the other neglecteth, in that contention all is subverted and cometh to ruin—in semblable[1] wise doth a public weal that hath more chief governors than one. Example we may take of the Greeks, among whom in divers cities were divers forms of public weals governed by multitudes; wherein one was most tolerable where the governance and rule was always permitted to them which excelled in virtue, and was in the Greek tongue called *aristocratia*, in Latin *optimorum potentia*, in English the rule of men of best disposition—which the Thebans of long time observed.

Another public weal was among the Athenians, where equality was of estate among the people, and only by their whole consent their city and dominions were governed; which might well be called a monster with many heads; nor never it was certain nor stable, and often-

[1] similar

times they banished or slew the best citizens which by their virtue and wisdom had most profited to the public weal. This manner of governance was called in Greek *democratia,* in Latin *popularis potentia,* in English the rule of the commonalty.

Of these two governances, none of them may be sufficient. For in the first, which consisteth of good men, virtue is not so constant in a multitude but that some being once in authority be incensed with glory; some with ambition; other with covetise[2] and desire of treasure or possessions, whereby they fall into contention; and finally, where any achieveth the superiority, the whole governance is reduced unto a few in number, which, fearing the multitude and their mutability, to the intent to keep them in dread to rebel, ruleth by terror and cruelty, thinking thereby to keep themself in surety; notwithstanding, rancor coarcted[3] and long detained in a narrow room, at the last bursteth out with intolerable violence and bringeth all to confusion. For the power that is practiced to the hurt of many cannot continue. The popular estate, if it anything do vary from equality of substance or estimation, or that the multitude of people have over-much liberty, of necessity one of these inconveniences must happen: either tyranny, where he that is too much in favor would be elevate and suffer none equality; or else into the rage of a commonalty, which of all rules is most to be feared. For like as the commons, if they feel some severity, they do humbly serve and obey, so where they, embracing a license, refuse to be bridled, they fling and plunge; and if they once throw down their governor, they order everything without justice, only with vengeance and cruelty; and with

[2] covetousness   [3] compressed

incomparable difficulty, and unneth[4] by any wisdom, be pacified and brought again into order.

Wherefore undoubtedly the best and most sure governance is by one king or prince, which ruleth only for the weal of his people to him subject; and that manner of governance is best approved, and hath longest continued, and is most ancient. For who can deny but that all thing in heaven and earth is governed by one God, by one perpetual order, by one providence? One sun ruleth over the day, and one moon over the night; and to descend down to the earth, in a little beast which of all other is most to be marveled at—I mean the bee—is left to man by nature, as it seemeth, a perpetual figure of a just governance or rule, who hath among them one principal bee for their governor, who excelleth all other in greatness, yet hath he no prick or sting, but in him is more knowledge than in the residue. For if the day following shall be fair and dry, and that the bees may issue out of their stalls without peril of rain or vehement wind, in the morning early he calleth them, making a noise as it were the sound of a horn or a trumpet; and with that, all the residue prepare them to labor, and fleeth abroad, gathering nothing but that shall be sweet and profitable, although they sit oftentimes on herbs and other things that be venomous and stinking. The captain himself laboreth not for his sustenance, but all the other for him; he only seeth that if any drone or other unprofitable bee entereth into the hive, and consumeth the honey gathered by other, that he be immediately expelled from that company. And when there is another number of bees increased, they semblably have also a captain, which be not suffered to continue with the other. Wherefore this new company, gathered into a swarm,

[4] scarcely

having their captain among them, and environing him to preserve him from harm, they issue forth seeking a new habitation, which they find in some tree, except with some pleasant noise they be allured and conveyed unto another hive.

I suppose who seriously beholdeth this example, and hath any commendable wit, shall thereof gather much matter to the forming of a public weal. But because I may not be long therein, considering my purpose, I would that if the reader hereof be learned, that he should repair to the *Georgics* of Virgil, or to Pliny, or Columella, where he shall find the example more ample and better declared. And if any desireth to have the governance of one person proved by histories, let him first resort to the Holy Scripture, where he shall find that Almighty God commanded Moses, only, to bring his elected people out of captivity, giving only to him that authority, without appointing to him any other assistance of equal power or dignity, except in the message to King Pharaoh, wherein Aaron rather as a minister than a companion went with Moses.

But only Moses conducted the people through the Red Sea; he only governed them forty years in desert. And because Dathan and Abiram disdained his rule, and coveted to be equal with him, the earth opened, and fire issued out, and swallowed them in, with all their whole family and confederates, to the number of 14,700. And although Jethro, Moses' father-in-law, counseled him to depart[5] his importable[6] labors in continual judgments unto the wise men that were in his company, he notwithstanding still retained the sovereignty, by God's commandment, until a little before he died he resigned it to Joshua, assigned by God to be ruler after him. Sem-

[5] share   [6] unendurable

blably after the death of Joshua, by the space of 246
years succeeded, from time to time, one ruler among the
Jews, which was chosen for his excellency in virtue, and
specially justice. Wherefore he was called the judge, until
the Israelites desired of Almighty God to let them have a
king, as other people had: who appointed to them Saul
to be their king, who exceeded all other in stature. And
so successively one king governed all the people of Israel
unto the time of Rehoboam son of the noble King Solomon, who, being unlike to his father in wisdom, practiced tyranny among his people. Wherefore nine parts
of them, which they called Tribes, forsook him, and
elected Jeroboam, late servant to Solomon, to be their
king, only the tenth part remaining with Rehoboam.

And so in that realm were continually two kings, until
the King of Media had depopulate[d] the country, and
brought the people in captivity to the city of Babylon.
So that during the time that two kings reigned over the
Jews was ever continual battle among themselves, where
if one king had always reigned like to David or Solomon,
of likelihood the country should not so soon have been
brought in captivity. Also in the time of the Maccabees,
as long as they had but one bishop, which was their ruler,
and was in the stead of a prince, at that day they valiantly
resisted the Gentiles; and as well the Romans, then great
lords of the world, as Persians and divers other realms
desired to have with them amity and alliance; and all the
inhabitants of that country lived in great weal[7] and quietness. But after that by simony and ambition there happened to be two bishops, which divided their authorities, and also the Romans had divided the realm of
Judea to four princes, called *tetrarchas,* and also constituted a Roman captain or president over them, among

[7] prosperity

the heads there never ceased to be sedition and perpetual discord; whereby at the last the people was destroyed, and the country brought to desolation and horrible barrenness.

The Greeks which were assembled to revenge the reproach of Menelaus, that he took of the Trojans by the ravishing of Helen his wife, did not they by one assent elect Agamemnon to be their emperor or captain, obeying him as their sovereign during the siege of Troy? Although that they had divers excellent princes not only equal to him but also excelling him (as in prowess Achilles and Ajax Thelemonius, in wisdom Nestor and Ulysses and his own brother, Menelaus) to whom they might have given equal authority with Agamemnon—but those wise princes considered that without a general captain, so many persons as were there, of divers realms gathered together, should be by no means well governed (wherefore Homer calleth Agamemnon the shepherd of people)—they rather were contented to be under one man's obedience than severally to use their authorities, or to join in one power and dignity, whereby at the last should have sourded[8] dissension among the people, they being separately inclined toward their natural sovereign lord, as it appeared in the particular contention that was between Achilles and Agamemnon for their concubines, where Achilles renouncing[9] the obedience that he with all other princes had before promised, at the battle first enterprised against the Trojans. For at that time no little murmur and sedition was moved in the host of the Greeks, which notwithstanding was wonderfully pacified, and the army unscattered, by the majesty of Agamemnon, joining to him counselors, Nestor and the witty Ulysses.

But to return again. Athens and other cities of Greece,

[8] arisen [9] that is, renounced

when they had abandoned kings, and concluded to live
as it were in a commonalty, which abusively they called
equality, how long time did any of them continue in
peace? Yea what vacation had they from the wars? Or
what nobleman had they, which advanced the honor and
weal of their city, whom they did not banish or slay in
prison? Surely it shall appear to them that will read
Plutarch or Aemilius Probus, in the lives of Miltiades,
Cimon, Themistocles, Aristides, and divers other noble
and valiant captains, which is too long here to rehearse.

In like wise the Romans, during the time that they
were under kings, which was by the space of 144 years,
were well governed, nor never was among them discord or
sedition. But after that by the persuasion of Brutus and
Collatinus, whose wife (Lucretia) was ravished by Arun-
cius, son of Tarquin, King of Romans, not only the said
Tarquin and all his posterity were exiled out of Rome
forever, but also it was finally determined among the
people that never after they would have a king reign
over them. Consequently the commonalty more and
more encroached[10] a license, and at the last compelled the
Senate to suffer them to choose yearly among them governors of their own estate and condition, whom they
called tribunes; under whom they received such audacity
and power that they finally obtained the highest authority in the public weal, in so much that often times they
did repeal the acts of the Senate, and to those tribunes
might a man appeal from the Senate, or any other office
or dignity. But what came thereof in conclusion? Surely
when there was any difficult war imminent, then were
they constrained to elect one sovereign and chief of all
other, whom they named *Dictator,* as it were commander,
from whom it was not lawful for any man to appeal. But

[10] seized

because there appeared to be in him the pristinate[11] authority and majesty of a king, they would no longer suffer him to continue in that dignity than by the space of six months, except he then resigned it, and by the consent of the people eftsoons[12] did resume it.

Finally until Octavius Augustus had destroyed Antony, and also Brutus, and finished all the Civil Wars (that were so called because they were between the same-self Roman citizens), the city of Rome was never long quiet from factions or seditions among the people. And if the nobles of Rome had not been men of excellent learning, wisdom, and prowess, and that the Senate—the most noble council in all the world, which was first ordained by Romulus, and increased by Tullus Hostilius, the third king of Romans—had not continued, and with great difficulty retained their authority, I suppose verily that the city of Rome had been utterly desolate[d] soon after the expelling of Tarquin. And if it had been eftsoons renewed, it should have been twenty times destroyed before the time that Augustus reigned, so much discord was ever in the city for lack of one governor.

But what need we to search so far from us, since we have sufficient examples near unto us? Behold the estate of Florence and Genoa, noble cities of Italy, what calamity have they both sustained by their own factions, for lack of a continual governor! Ferrara and the most excellent city of Venice, the one having a duke, the other an earl, seldom suffereth damage, except it happen by outward hostility. We have also an example domestical which is most necessary to be noted. After that the Saxons by treason had expelled out of England the Britons, which were the ancient inhabitants, this realm was divided into sundry regions, or kingdoms. O what misery

---

[11] pristine   [12] straightway

was the people then in! O how this most noble isle of
the world was decerpt[13] and rent in pieces—the people
pursued and hunted like wolves, or other beasts savage;
none industry availed, no strength defended, no riches
profited! Who would then have desired to have been
rather a man than a dog, when men either with sword
or with hunger perished, having no profit or sustenance
of their own corn or cattle, which by mutual war was
continually destroyed? Yet the dogs, either taking that
that men could not quietly come by, or feeding on the
dead bodies, which on every part lay scattered plente-
ously, did satisfy their hunger.

Where find ye any good laws that at that time were
made and used, or any commendable monument of any
science or craft in this realm occupied? Such iniquity
seemeth to be then that by the multitude of sovereign
governors all things had been brought to confusion, if
the noble king Edgar had not reduced the monarch to
his pristinate estate and figure; which brought to pass,
reason was revived, and people came to conformity, and
the realm began to take comfort, and to show some visage
of a public weal; and so (lauded be God) have continued,
but not being always in like estate or condition. Albeit it
is not to be despaired but that the king our sovereign
lord now reigning, and this realm always having one
prince, like unto his highness, equal to the ancient princes
in virtue and courage, it shall be reduced (God so dis-
posing) unto a public weal excelling all other in pre-
eminence of virtue and abundance of things necessary.

But for as much as I do well perceive that to write of
the office or duty of a sovereign governor or prince far
exceedeth the compass of my learning, Holy Scripture
affirming that the hearts of princes be in God's own hands

[13] plucked

and disposition, I will therefore keep my pen within the space that is described to me by the three noble masters, reason, learning, and experience. And by their enseign-ment[14] or teaching I will ordinately[15] treat of the two parts of a public weal, whereof the one shall be named Due Administration, the other Necessary Occupation, which shall be divided into two volumes. In the first shall be comprehended the best form of education or bringing up of noble children from their nativity, in such manner as they may be found worthy and also able to be governors of a public weal. The second volume, which God granting me quietness and liberty of mind I will shortly after send forth, it shall contain all the rem-nant which I can either by learning or experience find apt to the perfection of a just public weal. In the which I shall so endeavor myself that all men of what estate or condition soever they be shall find therein occasion to be always virtuously occupied; and not without pleasure, if they be not of the schools of Aristippus or Apicius, of whom the one supposed felicity to be only in lechery, the other in delicate feeding and gluttony; from whose sharp talons and cruel teeth I beseech all gentle readers to de-fend these works, which for their commodity is only compiled.

[14] instruction   [15] in order

3

That in a Public Weal Ought to Be Inferior Governors Called Magistrates, Which Shall Be Appointed or Chosen by the Sovereign Governor

There be both reasons and examples undoubtedly infinite whereby may be proved that there can be no perfect public weal, without one capital and sovereign governor, which may long endure or continue.

But since one mortal man cannot have knowledge of all things done in a realm or large dominion, and at one time discuss all controversies, reform all transgressions, and exploit all consultations, concluded as well for outward as inward affairs, it is expedient and also needful that under the capital governor be sundry mean authorities, as it were aiding him in the distribution of justice in sundry parts of a huge multitude; whereby his labors being levigate[1] and made more tolerable, he shall govern with the better advice, and consequently with a more perfect governance. And as Jesus Sirach saith: "The multitude of wise men is the wealth of the world." They which have such authorities to them committed may be called inferior governors, having respect to their office or duty, wherein is also a representation of governance, albeit they be named in Latin *magistratus*. And hereafter I intend to call them magistrates, lacking another more

[1] lightened

convenient word in English, but that will I do in the second part of this work, where I purpose to write of their sundry offices, or effects of their authority. But for as much as in this part I intend to write of their education and virtue in manners, which they have in common with princes, inasmuch as thereby they shall as well by example as by authority order well them which by their capital governor shall be to their rule committed, I may without annoyance of any man name them governors at this time, appropriating to the sovereigns names of kings and princes, since of a long custom these names in common form of speaking be in a higher pre-eminence and estimation than governors.

That in every common weal ought to be a great number of such manner of persons, it is partly proved in the chapter next before written, where I have spoken of the commodity of order. Also reason and common experience plainly declareth that where the dominion is large and populous, there is it convenient that a prince have many inferior governors, which be named of Aristotle his eyes, ears, hands, and legs; which if they be of the best sort (as he furthermore saith), it seemeth impossible a country not to be well governed by good laws. And except excellent virtue and learning do enable a man of the base estate of the commonalty to be thought of all men worthy to be so much advanced, else such governors would be chosen out of that estate of men which be called worshipful, if among them may be found a sufficient number ornate with virtue and wisdom, meet for such purpose; and that for sundry causes.

First it is of good congruence[2] that they which be superior in condition or havior[3] should have also pre-

<hr>

[2] fitness   [3] behavior

eminence in administration, if they be not inferior to other in virtue. Also they having of their own revenues certain, whereby they have competent substance to live without taking rewards, it is likely that they will not be so desirous of lucre (whereof may be engendered corruption) as they which have very little or nothing so certain.

Moreover where virtue is in a gentleman, it is commonly mixed with more sufferance, more affability, and mildness than for the more part it is in a person rural or of a very base lineage; and when it happeneth otherwise, it is to be accounted loathsome and monstrous. Furthermore where the person is worshipful, his governance, though it be sharp, is to the people more tolerable, and they therewith the less grutch[4] or be disobedient. Also such men having substance in goods by certain and stable possessions, which they may apportionate to their own living and bringing up of their children in learning and virtues, may (if nature repugn[5] not) cause them to be so instructed and furnished toward the administration of a public weal that a poor man's son, only by his natural wit, without other adminiculation[6] or aid, never or seldom may attain to the semblable.[7] Toward the which instruction I have with no little study and labors prepared this work, as almighty God be my judge, without arrogance or any spark of vainglory; but only to declare the fervent zeal that I have to my country, and that I desire only to employ that poor learning that I have gotten to the benefit thereof, and to the recreation of all the readers that be of any noble or gentle courage,[8] giving them occasion to eschew idleness, being occupied in reading this work, enfarced[9] thoroughly with such histories

---

[4] grumble   [5] oppose
[6] support   [7] like
[8] spirit   [9] stuffed

and sentences whereby they shall take (they themselves confessing) no little commodity if they will more than once or twice read it—the first reading being to them new, the second delicious, and every time after, more and more fruitful and excellent profitable.

4

The Education or Form of Bringing Up of the Child of a Gentleman Which Is to Have Authority in a Public Weal

For as much as all noble authors do conclude, and also common experience proveth, that where the governors of realms and cities be found adorned with virtues, and do employ their study and mind to the public weal, as well to the augmentation thereof as to the establishing and long continuance of the same, there a public weal must needs be both honorable and wealthy. To the intent that I will declare how such personages may be prepared, I will use the policy of a wise and cunning gardener, who purposing to have in his garden a fine and precious herb, that should be to him and all other repairing thereto excellently commodious or pleasant, he will first search throughout his garden where he can find the most mellow and fertile earth, and therein will he put the seed of the herb to grow and be nourished; and in most diligent wise attend that no weed be suffered to grow or approach nigh unto it; and to the intent it may thrive the faster, as soon as the form of an herb once appeareth, he will set a vessel of water by it, in such wise that it may continually distill on the root sweet drops; and as it springeth in stalk, underset it with some thing, that it break not; and alway keep it clean from weeds. Semblable[1] order will I ensue[2]

[1] Similar   [2] pursue

in the forming the gentle wits of noblemen's children who, from the wombs of their mother, shall be made propise[3] or apt to the governance of a public weal.

First they unto whom the bringing up of such children appertaineth ought, against the time that their mother shall be of them delivered, to be sure of a nurse which should be of no servile condition or vice notable. For as some ancient writers do suppose, oftentimes the child sucketh the vice of his nurse with the milk of her pap. And also observe that she be of mature or ripe age, not under twenty years or above thirty, her body also being clean from all sickness or deformity, and having her complexion most of the right and pure sanguine, for as much as the milk thereof coming excelleth all other both in sweetness and substance. Moreover to the nurse should be appointed another woman of approved virtue, discretion, and gravity who shall not suffer in the child's presence to be showed any act or tache[4] dishonest, or any wanton or unclean word to be spoken; and for that cause all men, except physicians only, should be excluded and kept out of the nursery. Perchance some will scorn me for that I am so serious, saying that there is no such damage to be feared in an infant, who for tenderness of years hath not the understanding to discern good from evil. And yet no man will deny but in that innocency he will discern milk from butter, and bread from pap, and ere he can speak, he will with his hand or countenance signify which he desireth. And I verily do suppose that in the brains and hearts of children, which be members spiritual while they be tender and the little slips of reason begin in them to burgeon, there may hap by evil custom some pestiferous dew of vice to pierce the said members, and infect and corrupt the soft and tender

[3] fit (Fr., *propice*)   [4] trait

buds, whereby the fruit may grow wild, and some time
contain in it fervent and mortal poison, to the utter destruction of a realm.

And we have in daily experience that little infants
assayeth[5] to follow, not only the words but also the
faictes[6] and gesture of them that be provect[7] in years.
For we daily hear, to our great heaviness, children swear
great oaths and speak lascivious and unclean words by
the example of other whom they hear, whereat the lewd[8]
parents do rejoice—soon after, or[9] in this world, or else-
where, to their great pain and torment. Contrariwise we
behold some children, kneeling in their game before
images and holding up their little white hands, do move
their pretty mouths as they were praying; other going
and singing, as it were in procession. Whereby they do
express their disposition to the imitation of those things,
be they good or evil, which they usually do see or hear.
Wherefore not only princes but also all other children,
from their nurses' paps, are to be kept diligently from
the hearing or seeing of any vice or evil tache. And in-
continent[10] as soon as they can speak, it behooveth with
most pleasant allurings to instill in them sweet manners
and virtuous custom. Also to provide for them such companions and playfellows which shall not do in his presence any reproachable act or speak any unclean word or
oath, nor to advaunt[11] him with flattery, remembering
his nobility or any other like thing wherein he might
glory—unless it be to persuade him to virtue or to withdraw him from vice, in the remembering to him the danger of his evil, example. For noblemen more grievously

[5] try
[6] acts (Fr., *fait*)
[7] advanced
[8] ignorant
[9] either
[10] immediately
[11] inflate (Fr., *vanter*)

offend by their example than by their deed. Yet often remembrance to them of their estate may happen to radicate[12] in their hearts intolerable pride, the most dangerous poison to nobleness. Wherefore there is required to be therein much cautele[13] and soberness.

[12] root   [13] caution

5

The Order of Learning That a Nobleman Should Be Trained in Before He Come to the Age of Seven Years

Some old authors hold opinion that before the age of seven years a child should not be instructed in letters; but those writers were either Greeks or Latins, among whom all doctrine and sciences were in their maternal tongues, by reason whereof they saved all that long time which at this day is spent in understanding perfectly the Greek or Latin. Wherefore it requireth now a longer time to the understanding of both. Therefore that infelicity of our time and country compelleth us to encroach somewhat upon the years of children, and specially of noblemen, that they may sooner attain to wisdom and gravity than private persons, considering as I have said their charge and example, which above all things is most to be esteemed. Notwithstanding I would not have them enforced by violence to learn, but according to the counsel of Quintilian, to be sweetly allured thereto with praises and such pretty gifts as children delight in. And their first letters to be painted or limned in a pleasant manner, wherein children of gentle courage[1] have much delectation. And also there is no better allective[2] to noble wits than to induce them into a contention with their inferior companions, they sometime purposely suffering

<hr />

[1] spirit   [2] enticement

the more noble children to vanquish, and as it were giving to them place and sovereignty, though indeed the inferior children have more learning. But there can be nothing more convenient than by little and little to train and exercise them in speaking of Latin: informing them to know first the names in Latin of all things that cometh in sight, and to name all the parts of their bodies; and giving them somewhat that they covet or desire, in most gentle manner to teach them to ask it again in Latin. And if by this means they may be induced to understand and speak Latin, it shall afterward be less grief to them, in a manner, to learn anything where they understand the language wherein it is written. And as touching grammar, there is at this day better introductions, and more facile,[3] than ever before were made, concerning as well Greek as Latin, if they be wisely chosen.

And it shall be no reproach to a nobleman to instruct his own children, or at the least ways to examine them by way of dalliance[4] or solace,[5] considering that the emperor Octavius Augustus disdained not to read the works of Cicero and Virgil to his children and nephews. And why should not noblemen rather so do than teach their children how at dice and cards they may cunningly lose and consume their own treasure and substance? Moreover teaching representeth the authority of a prince; wherefore Dionysius King of Sicily, when he was for tyranny expelled by his people, he came into Italy, and there in a common school taught grammar, wherewith when he was of his enemies embraided[6] and called a schoolmaster, he answered them: that although Sicilians had exiled him, yet in despite of them all he reigned, noting thereby the authority that he had over his schol-

---

[3] more easily understood
[5] amusement, recreation
[4] sport, play
[6] upbraided

ars. Also when it was of him demanded what availed him Plato, or philosophy, wherein he had been studious, he answered that they caused him to sustain adversity patiently, and made his exile to be to him more facile and easy. Which courage and wisdom considered of his people, they eftsoons[7] restored him unto his realm and estate royal, where if he had procured against them hostility or wars, or had returned into Sicily with any violence, I suppose the people would have always resisted him, and have kept him in perpetual exile—as the Romans did the proud king Tarquin, whose son ravished Lucrece.

But to return to my purpose: it shall be expedient that a nobleman's son in his infancy have with him continually only such as may accustom him by little and little to speak pure and elegant Latin. Semblably[8] the nurses and other women about him, if it be possible, to do the same—or at the least way, that they speak none English but that which is clean, polite, perfectly and articulately pronounced, omitting no letter or syllable, as foolish women oftentimes do of a wantonness, whereby divers noblemen and gentlemen's children (as I do at this day know) have attained corrupt and foul pronunciation. This industry used in forming little infants, who shall doubt but that they (not lacking natural wit) shall be apt to receive learning when they come to more years? And in this wise may they be instructed without any violence or enforcing, using the more part of the time until they come to the age of seven years in such disports[9] as do appertain to children, wherein is no resemblance or similitude of vice.

[7] straightway   [8] Similarly
[9] pastimes

6

At What Age a Tutor Should Be Provided, and What Shall Appertain to His Office to Do

After that a child is come to seven years of age, I hold it expedient[1] that he be taken from the company of women, saving that he may have one year or two at the most an ancient and sad matron attending on him in his chamber, which shall not have any young woman in her company; for though there be no peril of offense in that tender and innocent age, yet in some children nature is more prone to vice than to virtue, and in the tender wits be sparks of voluptuosity which, nourished by any occasion or object, increase oftentimes into so terrible a fire that therewith all virtue and reason is consumed. Wherefore to eschew that danger, the most sure counsel is to withdraw him from all company of women, and to assign unto him a tutor, which should be an ancient and worshipful man in whom is approved to be much gentleness mixed with gravity, and, as nigh as can be, such one as the child, by imitation following, may grow to be excellent. And if he be also learned, he is the more commendable. Peleus the father of Achilles committed the governance of his son to Phoenix, which was a stranger born, who as well in speaking elegantly as in doing val-

[1] proper

iantly was master to Achilles (as Homer saith). How
much profited it to King Philip, father to the great Alexander, that he was delivered in hostage to the Thebans!
Where he was kept and brought up under the governance
of Epaminondas, a noble and valiant captain, of whom
he received such learning, as well in acts martial as in
other liberal sciences, that he excelled all other kings that
were before his time in Greece; and finally as well by
wisdom as prowess subdued all that country.

Semblably[2] he ordained for his son Alexander a noble
tutor, called Leonidas, unto whom for his wisdom, humanity, and learning he committed the rule and pre-
eminence over all the masters and servants of Alexander.
In whom notwithstanding was such a familiar vice, which
Alexander apprehending[3] in childhood could never abandon: some suppose it to be fury and hastiness, other superfluous drinking of wine; which of them it were, it is
a good warning for gentlemen to be the more serious in
searching not only for the virtues but also for the vices
of them unto whose tuition and governance they will
commit their children.

The office of a tutor is first to know the nature of his
pupil—that is to say, whereto he is most inclined or disposed, and in what thing he setteth his most delectation[4]
or appetite. If he be of nature courteous, piteous,[5] and of
a free and liberal heart, it is a principal token of grace
(as it is by all Scripture determined). Then shall a wise
tutor purposely commend those virtues, extolling also
his pupil for having of them; and therewith he shall declare them to be of all men most fortunate which shall
happen to have such a master. And moreover shall de-

---

[2] Similarly   [3] learning
[4] delight   [5] godly

clare to him what honor, what love, what commodity[6] shall happen to him by these virtues. And if any have been of disposition contrary, then to express the enormities of their vice, with as much detestation as may be. And if any danger have thereby ensued, misfortune, or punishment, to aggrieve it[7] in such wise, with so vehement words, as the child may abhor it and fear the semblable adventure.

[6] advantage [7] to make it worse

7

In What Wise Music May Be to a Nobleman Necessary, and What Modesty Ought to Be Therein

The discretion of a tutor consisteth in temperance: that is to say, that he suffer not the child to be fatigate[1] with continual study or learning, wherewith the delicate and tender wit may be dulled or oppressed; but that there may be therewith interlaced and mixed some pleasant learning and exercise, as playing on instruments of music, which, moderately used, and without diminution of honor—that is to say, without wanton countenance and dissolute gesture—is not to be contemned. For the noble king and prophet David, King of Israel (whom Almighty God said that he had chosen as a man according to his heart or desire), during his life delighted in music. And with the sweet harmony that he made on his harp, he constrained the evil spirit that vexed King Saul to forsake him, continuing the time that he harped. The most noble and valiant princes of Greece oftentimes, to recreate their spirits, and in augmenting their courage, embraced instruments musical. So did the valiant Achilles (as Homer saith) [who[2]] after the sharp and vehement contention between him and Agamemnon for the taking

[1] fatigued
[2] In order to make syntactical sense of this "sentence" and the two sentences following, the reader should ignore this pronoun.

away of his concubine, whereby he, being set in a fury,
had slain Agamemnon emperor of the Greeks' army, had
not Pallas the goddess withdrawn his hand. In which
rage he all inflamed departed with his people to his own
ships, that lay at rode,[3] intending to have returned into
his country; but after that he had taken to him his harp
(whereon he had learned to play of Chiron the centaur,
which also had taught him feats of arms, with physic and
surgery), and playing thereon had sung the gests and acts
martial of the ancient princes of Greece (as Hercules,
Perseus, Pirithous, Theseus, and his cousin Jason) and
of divers other of semblable[4] value and prowess, he was
therewith assuaged of his fury and reduced into his first
estate of reason; in such wise that in redoubing[5] his rage,
and that thereby should not remain to him any note of
reproach, he, retaining his fierce and sturdy countenance,
so tempered himself in the entertainment and answering
the messengers that came to him from the residue of the
Greeks that they, reputing all that his fierce demeanor
to be (as it were) a divine majesty, never embraided[6] him
with any inordinate wrath or fury.

And therefore the great King Alexander, when he had
vanquished Ilion, where some time was set the most
noble city of Troy, being demanded of one if he would
see the harp of Paris Alexander, who ravished Helen, he,
thereat gently smiling, answered: that it was not the
thing that he much desired, but that he had rather see
the harp of Achilles whereto he sang, not the illecebrous[7]
dilectations[8] of Venus, but the valiant acts and noble
affairs of excellent princes. But in this commendation of
music, I would not be thought to allure noblemen to

---

[3] roadstead, harbor   [4] like
[5] repairing (Fr., *radouber*)   [6] upbraided
[7] alluring   [8] delights

have so much dilectation therein that in playing and singing only, they should put their whole study and feliccity. As did the emperor Nero, which all a long summer's day would sit in the Theatre (an open place where all the people of Rome beheld solemn acts and plays), and in the presence of all the noblemen and senators would play on his harp and sing without ceasing. And if any man happened by long sitting to sleep, or by any other countenance to show himself to be weary, he was suddenly bobbed on the face by the servants of Nero, for that purpose attending. Or if any person were perceived to be absent, or were seen to laugh at the folly of the emperor, he was forthwith accused as it were of misprision, whereby the emperor found occasion to commit him to prison, or to put him to tortures. O what misery was it to be subject to such a minstrel, in whose music was no melody but anguish and dolor!

It were therefore better that no music were taught to a nobleman than by the exact knowledge thereof he should have therein inordinate delight; and by that be illected[9] to wantonness, abandoning gravity and the necessary cure[10] and office in the public weal to him committed. King Philip, when he heard that his son Alexander did sing sweetly and properly, he rebuked him gently, saying: "But Alexander, be ye not ashamed that ye can sing so well and cunningly?" Whereby he meant that the open profession of that craft was but of a base estimation; and that it sufficed a nobleman, having therein knowledge, either to use it secretly, for the refreshing of his wit, when he hath time of solace, or else, only hearing the contention[11] of noble musicians, to give judgment in the excellency of their cunnings.

[9] enticed   [10] care
[11] striving

These be the causes, whereunto having regard, music is not only tolerable but also commendable. For as Aristotle saith, music in the old time was numbered among sciences, for as much as nature seeketh not only how to be in business well occupied, but also how in quietness to be commendably disposed. And if the child be of a perfect inclination and towardness to virtue, and very aptly disposed to this science, and ripely doth understand the reason and concordance of tunes, the tutor's office shall be to persuade him to have principally in remembrance his estate, which maketh him exempt from the liberty of using this science in every time and place; that is to say, that it only serveth for recreation after tedious or laborious affairs. And to show him that a gentleman playing or singing in a common audience appaireth[12] his estimation, the people forgetting reverence when they behold him in the similitude of a common servant or minstrel.

Yet notwithstanding, he shall commend the perfect understanding of music, declaring how necessary it is for the better attaining the knowledge of a public weal, which, as I before have said, is made of an order of estates and degrees, and by reason thereof containeth in it a perfect harmony; which he shall afterward more perfectly understand when he shall happen to read the books of Plato and Aristotle of public weals, wherein be written divers examples of music and geometry. In this form may a wise and circumspect tutor adapt the pleasant science of music to a necessary and laudable purpose.

[12] impairs

8

That It Is Commendable in a Gentleman
to Paint and Carve Exactly, If Nature
Thereto Doth Induce Him

If the child be of nature inclined (as many have been) to paint with a pen or to form images in stone or tree, he should not be therefrom withdrawn, or nature be rebuked, which is to him benevolent; but putting one to him which is in that craft wherein he delighteth most excellent, in vacant times from other more serious learning he should be in the most pure wise instructed in painting or carving.

And now perchance some envious reader will hereof apprehend occasion to scorn me, saying that I have well hyed me[1] to make of a nobleman a mason or painter. And yet if either ambition or voluptuous idleness would have suffered that reader to have seen histories, he should have found excellent princes, as well in painting as in carving, equal to noble artificers; such were Claudius Titus, the son of Vespasian, Hadrian, both Antonines, and divers other emperors and noble princes, whose works of long time remained in Rome and other cities, in such places where all men might behold them, as monuments of their excellent wits and virtuous occupation in eschewing of idleness. And not without a necessary cause princes were in their childhood so instructed,

[1] striven

for it served them afterward for devising of engines for
the war, or for making them better that be already devised. For as Vitruvius (which writeth of building to the
emperor Augustus) saith, all turments[2] of war, which we
call ordnance, were first invented by kings or governors
of hosts; or, if they were devised by other, they were by
them made much better.

Also by the feat of portraiture or painting, a captain
may describe the country of his adversary, whereby he
shall eschew the dangerous passages with his host or navy;
also perceive the places of advantage, the form of embattling of his enemies, the situation of his camp for his
most surety, the strength or weakness of the town or
fortress which he intendeth to assault. And that which
is most specially to be considered, in visiting his own
dominions he shall set them out in figure in such wise
that at his eye shall appear to him where he shall employ
his study and treasure, as well for the safeguard of his
country as for the commodity and honor thereof, having
at all times in his sight the surety and feebleness, advancement and hindrance of the same.

And what pleasure and also utility is it to a man which
intendeth to edify,[3] himself to express the figure of the
work that he purposeth, according as he hath conceived
it in his own fantasy! Wherein by often amending and
correcting, he finally shall so perfect the work unto his
purpose that there shall neither ensue any repentance,
nor in the employment of his money he shall be by other
deceived. Moreover the feat of portraiture shall be an
allective[4] to every other study or exercise. For the wit
thereto disposed shall alway covet congruent matter
wherein it may be occupied. And when he happeneth to

[2] engines   [3] build
[4] enticement

read or hear any fable or history, forthwith he appre-
hendeth it more desirously and retaineth it better than
any other that lacketh the said feat, by reason that he
hath found matter apt to his fantasy. Finally every thing
that portraiture may comprehend will be to him delectable to read or hear. And where the lively spirit, and
that which is called the grace of the thing, is perfectly expressed, that thing more persuadeth and stirreth the be-
holder, and sooner instructeth him than the declaration
in writing or speaking doth the reader or hearer.

Experience we have thereof in learning of geometry,
astronomy, and cosmography, called in English the description of the world. In which studies, I dare affirm, a
man shall more profit in one week by figures and charts,
well and perfectly made, than he shall by the only reading or hearing the rules of that science by the space of
half a year at the least. Wherefore the late writers de-
serve no small commendation, which added to the authors of those sciences apt and proper figures.

And he that is perfectly instructed in portraiture, and
happeneth to read any noble and excellent history
whereby his courage[5] is inflamed to the imitation of
virtue, he forthwith taketh his pen or pencil, and with a
grave and substantial study, gathering to him all the
parts of imagination, endeavoreth himself to express
lively, and (as I might say) actually in portraiture, not
only the faict[6] or affair, but also the sundry affections[7] of
every personage in the history recited which might in any
wise appear or be perceived in their visage, countenance,
or gesture—with like diligence as Lysippus made in metal
King Alexander, fighting and struggling with a terrible

[5] spirit   [6] deed
[7] emotions

lion of incomparable magnitude and fierceness, whom, after long and difficult battle, with wonderful strength and clean might at the last he overthrew and vanquished. Wherein he so expressed the similitude of Alexander, and of his lords standing about him, that they all seemed to live. Among whom the prowess of Alexander appeared excelling all other, the residue of his lords after the value and estimation of their courage, every man set out in such forwardness as they then seemed more prompt to the helping of their master—that is to say, one less afeared than another. Phidias the Athenian, whom all writers do commend, made of ivory the simulacrum or image of Jupiter, honored by the Gentiles, on the high hill of Olympus; which was done so excellently that Pandenus, a cunning painter, thereat admarveling, required the craftsman to show him where he had the example or pattern of so noble a work. Then Phidias answered, that he had taken it out of three verses of Homer the poet; the sentence[8] whereof ensueth as well as my poor wit can express it in English:

> Then Jupiter, the father of them all,
> Thereto assented with his brows black,
> Shaking his hair, and therewith did let fall
> A countenance that made all heaven to quake—

where it is to be noted that Homer immediately before had rehearsed the consultation had among the gods for the appeasing of the two noble princes, Achilles and Agamemnon.

Now (as I have before said) I intend not by these examples to make of a prince or nobleman's son a common painter or carver, which shall present himself openly,

[8] sense

stained or embrued with sundry colors, or powdered with
the dust of stones that he cutteth, or perfumed with tedious[9] savors[10] of the metals by him yoten.[11] But verily
mine intent and meaning is only that a noble child, by
his own natural disposition, and not by coercion, may be
induced to receive perfect instruction in these sciences.
But although, for purposes before expressed, they shall
be necessary, yet shall they not be by him exercised but as
a secret pastime, or recreation of the wits late occupied
in serious studies, like as did the noble princes before
named. Although they once being attained, be never
much exercised after that the time cometh concerning
business of greater importance, nevertheless the exquisite
knowledge and understanding that he hath in those sciences hath impressed in his ears and eyes an exact and
perfect judgment, as well in discerning the excellency of
them which either in music, or in statuary, or painters'
craft professeth any cunning, as also adapting their said
knowledge to the adminiculation[12] of other serious studies and business, as I have before rehearsed. Which I
doubt not shall be well approved by them that either
have read and understand old authors, or advisedly will
examine my considerations.

The sweet writer Lactantius saith in his first book to
the emperor Constantine against the Gentiles: "Of cunning cometh virtue, and of virtue perfect felicity is only
engendered." And for that cause the Gentiles supposed
those princes which in virtue and honor surmounted
other men to be gods. And the Romans in like wise did
consecrate their emperors which excelled in virtuous example, in preserving or augmenting the public weal and

---

[9] disagreeable   [10] smells
[11] cast   [12] support

ampliating[13] of the empire, calling them *divi;* which word representeth a signification of divinity, they thinking that it was exceeding man's nature to be both in fortune and goodness of such perfection.

[13] enlarging

What Exact Diligence Should Be
in Choosing Masters

After that the child hath been pleasantly trained and induced to know the parts of speech, and can separate one
of them from another in his own language, it shall then
be time that his tutor or governor do make diligent
search for such a master as is excellently learned both in
Greek and Latin, and therewithal is of sober and virtuous
disposition, specially chaste of living and of much affability and patience—lest by any unclean example the
tender mind of the child may be infected, hard afterward
to be recovered. For the natures of children be not so
much or soon advanced by things well done or spoken
as they be hindered and corrupted by that which in acts
or words is wantonly expressed. Also by a cruel and
irous[1] master the wits of children be dulled; and that
thing for the which children be oftentimes beaten is to
them ever after fastidious,[2] whereof we need no better
author for witness than daily experience. Wherefore the
most necessary things to be observed by a master in his
disciples or scholars (as Lycon the noble grammarian
saith) is shamefastness and praise. By shamefastness, as it
were with a bridle, they rule as well their deeds as their
appetites. And desire of praise addeth to a sharp spur

[1] irascible   [2] disgusting

to their disposition toward learning and virtue. Accord ing thereunto Quintilian, instructing an orator, desireth such a child to be given unto him whom commendation fervently stirreth, glory provoketh, and being vanquished weepeth. That child (saith he) is to be fed with ambition, him a little chiding sore biteth, in him no part of sloth is to be feared.

And if nature disposeth not the child's wit to receive learning, but rather otherwise, it is to be applied with more diligence and also policy, as choosing some book whereof the argument or matter approacheth most nigh to the child's inclination or fantasy, so that it be not extremely vicious, and therewith by little and little, as it were with a pleasant sauce, provoke him to have good appetite to study. And surely that child, whatsoever he be, is well blessed and fortunate that findeth a good instructor or master. Which was considered by noble King Philip, father to the great King Alexander, who immediately after that his son was born, wrote a letter to Aristotle, the prince of philosophers, the tenor whereof ensueth.

"Aristotle, we greet you well. Letting you weete[3] that we have a son born, for the which we give due thanks unto God, not for that he is born only, but also for as much as it happeneth him to be born, you living. Trusting that it shall happen that he by you taught and instructed, shall be hereafter worthy to be named our son, and to enjoy the honor and substance that we now have provided. Thus fare ye well."

The same Alexander was wont to say openly that he ought to give as great thanks to Aristotle his master as to King Philip his father, for of him he took the occasion to live, of the other he received the reason and way to

[3] know

live well. And what manner a prince Alexander was
made by the doctrine of Aristotle, it shall appear in divers
places of this book, where his example to princes shall be
declared. The incomparable benefit of masters have been
well remembered of divers princes. In so much as Marcus
Antoninus, which among the emperors was commended
for his virtue and sapience, had his master Proculus (who
taught him grammar) so much in favor that he advanced
him to be proconsul, which was one of the highest dignities among the Romans. Alexander the emperor caused
his master Julius Fronto[4] to be consul, which was the
highest office, and in estate next the emperor; and also
obtained of the Senate that the statue or image of Fronto
was set up among the noble princes.

What caused Trajan to be so good a prince, in so much
that of late days, when an emperor received his crown at
Rome, the people with a common cry desired of God that
he might be as good as was Trajan, but that he happened
to have Plutarch the noble philosopher to be his instructor? I agree me that some be good of natural inclination to goodness; but where good instruction and
example is thereto added, the natural goodness must
therewith needs be amended, and be more excellent.

[4] Elyot is in error. Sextus Julius Frontinus (c. A.D. 30–104)
tutored Alexander Severus in rhetoric; Marcus Cornelius Fronto
(c. A.D. 100–c. 166) tutored Marcus Aurelius and Lucius Verus in
the same subject.

10

What Order Should Be in Learning, and Which Authors Should Be First Read

Now let us return to the order of learning apt for a gentleman. Wherein I am of the opinion of Quintilian, that I would have him learn Greek and Latin authors both at one time; or else to begin with Greek, for as much as that it is hardest to come by, by reason of the diversity of tongues, which be five in number; and all must be known, or else uneth[1] any poet can be well understand. And if a child do begin therein at seven years of age, he may continually learn Greek authors three years, and in the meantime use the Latin tongue as a familiar language —which in a nobleman's son may well come to pass, having none other persons to serve him or keeping him company but such as can speak Latin elegantly. And what doubt is there but so may he as soon speak good Latin as he may do pure French, which now is brought into as many rules and figures, and as long a grammar, as is Latin or Greek? I will not contend who among them that do write grammars of Greek (which now almost be innumerable) is the best; but that I refer to the discretion of a wise master. Alway I would advise him not to detain the child too long in that tedious labors, either in the Greek or Latin grammar. For a gentle wit is therewith soon fatigate.[2]

[1] hardly   [2] fatigued

Grammar being but an introduction to the understanding of authors, if it be made too long or exquisite to the learner, it in a manner mortifieth his courage.[3] And by that time he cometh to the most sweet and pleasant reading of old authors, the sparks of fervent desire of learning is extinct with the burden of grammar, like as a little fire is soon quenched with a great heap of small sticks, so that it can never come to the principal logs, where it should long burn in a great pleasant fire.

Now to follow my purpose: after a few and quick rules of grammar, immediately or interlacing it therewith would be read to the child Aesop's fables in Greek, in which argument children much do delight. And surely it is a much pleasant lesson and also profitable, as well for that it is elegant and brief (and notwithstanding it hath much variety in words, and therewith much helpeth to the understanding of Greek) as also in those fables is included much moral and politic wisdom. Wherefore in the teaching of them, the master diligently must gather together those fables which may be most accommodate to the advancement of some virtue whereto he perceiveth the child inclined, or to the rebuke of some vice whereto he findeth his nature disposed. And therein the master ought to exercise his wit, as well to make the child plainly to understand the fable, as also declaring the signification thereof compendiously and to the purpose. Foreseen[4] alway that as well this lesson as all other authors which the child shall learn, either Greek or Latin, verse or prose, be perfectly had without the book; whereby he shall not only attain plenty of the tongues called copie,[5] but also increase and nourish remembrance wonderfully. The next lesson would be some quick and merry dia-

[3] spirit   [4] foreseeing (?)
[5] *copia*

logues elect out of Lucian which be without ribaldry or
too much scorning, for either of them is exactly to be
eschewed, specially for a nobleman, the one annoying the
soul, the other his estimation concerning his gravity. The
comedies of Aristophanes may be in the place of Lucian;
and by reason that they be in meter, they be the sooner
learned by heart. I dare make none other comparison between them, for offending the friends of them both; but
thus much dare I say, that it were better that a child
should never read any part of Lucian than all Lucian.

I could rehearse divers other poets which for matter
and eloquence be very necessary, but I fear me to be too
long from noble Homer, from whom, as from a fountain,
proceeded all eloquence and learning. For in his books
be contained, and more perfectly expressed, not only the
documents martial and discipline of arms, but also incomparable wisdoms, and instructions for politic governance
of people, with the worthy commendation and laud of
noble princes; wherewith the readers shall be so all inflamed that they most fervently shall desire and covet, by
the imitation of their virtues, to acquire semblable[6] glory.
For the which occasion Aristotle, most sharpest witted
and excellent learned philosopher, as soon as he had received Alexander from King Philip his father, he before
any other thing taught him the most noble works of
Homer. Wherein Alexander found such sweetness and
fruit that ever after he had Homer not only with him in
all his journeys, but also laid him under his pillow when
he went to rest; and oftentimes would purposely wake
some hours of the night to take as it were his pastime
with that most noble poet. For by the reading of his
work called *Iliados,* where the assembly of the most noble
Greeks against Troy is recited with their affairs, he gath-

[6] similar

ered courage and strength against his enemies, wisdom
and eloquence for consultations and persuasions to his
people and army. And by the other work called *Odissea*,
which recounteth the sundry adventures of the wise
Ulysses, he by the example of Ulysses apprehended many
noble virtues, and also learned to escape the fraud and
deceitful imaginations of sundry and subtle crafty wits.
Also there shall he learn to ensearch and perceive the
manners and conditions of them that be his familiars,
sifting out (as I might say) the best from the worst,
whereby he may surely commit his affairs and trust to
every person after his virtues.

Therefore I now conclude that there is no lesson for
a young gentleman to be compared with Homer, if he be
plainly and substantially expounded and declared by the
master.

Notwithstanding, for as much as the said works be very
long, and do require therefore a great time to be all
learned and conned, some Latin author would be therewith mixed, and specially Virgil; which in his work
called *Eneidos* is most like to Homer, and almost the
same Homer in Latin. Also by the joining together of
those authors, the one shall be the better understand by
the other. And verily (as I before said) none one author
serveth to so divers wits as doth Virgil. For there is not
that affect[7] or desire whereto any child's fantasy is disposed, but in some of Virgil's works may be found matter
thereto apt and propise.[8] For what thing can be more
familiar than his *Bucolics*? Nor no work so nigh approacheth to the common dalliance[9] and manners of
children; and the pretty controversies of the simple shep-
herds therein contained wonderfully rejoiceth the child

---

[7] natural tendency   [8] fit
[9] play

that heareth it well declared, as I know by mine own experience. In his *Georgics,* Lord what pleasant variety there is—the divers grains, herbs, and flowers that be there described—that reading therein it seemeth to a man to be in a delectable garden or paradise! What plowman knoweth so much of husbandry as there is expressed? Who delighting in good horses shall not be thereto more enflamed, reading there of the breeding, choosing, and keeping of them? In the declaration whereof, Virgil leaveth far behind him all breeders, hackney[10] men, and skosers.[11] Is there any astronomer that more exactly setteth out the order and course of the celestial bodies, or that more truly doth divine in his prognostications of the times of the year, in their qualities, with the future estate of all things provided by husbandry, than Virgil doth recite in that work?

If the child have a delight in hunting, what pleasure shall he take of the fable of Aristaeus; semblably in the hunting of Dido and Aeneas, which is described most elegantly in his book of *Eneidos!* If he have pleasure in wrestling, running, or other like exercise, where shall he see any more pleasant esbatementes[12] than that which was done by Euryalus and other Trojans which accompanied Aeneas! If he take solace in hearing minstrels, what minstrel may be compared to Iopas, which sang before Dido and Aeneas! Or to blind Demodocus, that played and sang most sweetly at the dinner that the King Alcinous made to Ulysses, whose ditties and melody excelled as far the songs of our minstrels as Homer and Virgil excel all other poets!

If he be more desirous (as the most part of children

[10] a horse used for ordinary riding
[11] skorsers (scorsers)—horse dealers
[12] amusements

be) to hear things marvelous and exquisite, which hath
in it a visage of some things incredible, whereat shall be
more wonder than when he shall behold Aeneas follow
Sibyl into hell! What shall he more dread than the terrible visages of Cerberus, Gorgon, Megaera, and other
furies and monsters! How shall he abhor tyranny, fraud,
and avarice when he doth see the pains of Duke Theseus,
Prometheus, Sisyphus, and such other, tormented for
their dissolute and vicious living! How glad soon after
shall he be when he shall behold in the pleasant fields of
Elysium the souls of noble princes and captains, which,
for their virtue and labors in advancing the public weals
of their countries, do live eternally in pleasure inexplicable! And in the last books of *Eneidos* shall he find matter to minister to him audacity, valiant courage, and
policy, to take and sustain noble enterprises, if any shall
be needful for the assailing of his enemies. Finally (as I
have said) this noble Virgil, like to a good nurse, giveth
to a child, if he will take it, everything apt for his wit
and capacity. Wherefore he is in the order of learning to
be preferred before any other author Latin.

I would set next unto him two books of Ovid, the one
called *Metamorphosios,* which is as much to say as, chang-
ing of men into other figure or form; the other is entitled
De fastis, where the ceremonies of the Gentiles, and specially the Romans, be expressed—both right necessary
for the understanding of other poets. But because there
is little other learning in them concerning either virtuous
manners or policy, I suppose it were better that, as fables
and ceremonies happen to come in a lesson, it were declared abundantly by the master, than that in the said
two books a long time should be spent and almost lost
which might be better employed on such authors that do

minister both eloquence, civil policy, and exhortation to virtue.

Wherefore in his place let us bring in Horace, in whom is contained much variety of learning and quickness of sentence.[13] This poet may be interlaced with the lesson of *Odissea* of Homer, wherein is declared the wonderful prudence and fortitude of Ulysses in his passage from Troy.

And if the child were induced to make verses by the imitation of Virgil and Homer, it should minister to him much delectation and courage[14] to study; ne[15] the making of verses is not discommended in a nobleman, since the noble Augustus and almost all the old emperors made books in verses.

The two noble poets Silius and Lucan be very expedient to be learned, for the one setteth out the emulation in qualities and prowess of two noble and valiant captains, one enemy to the other: that is to say, Silius writeth of Scipio the Roman and Hannibal Duke of Carthage; Lucan declareth a semblable matter, but much more lamentable, for as much as the wars were civil, and as it were in the bowels of the Romans, that is to say, under the standards of Julius Caesar and Pompey.

Hesiod in Greek is more brief than Virgil where he writeth of husbandry, and doth not rise so high in philosophy, but is fuller of fables, and therefore is more illecebrous.[16]

And here I conclude to speak any more of poets necessary for the childhood of a gentleman, for as much as these I doubt not will suffice until he pass the age of thirteen years. In which time childhood declineth, and

[13] thought
[15] nor
[14] enthusiasm
[16] alluring

reason waxeth ripe, and deprehendeth[17] things with a more constant judgment.

Here I would should be remembered that I require not that all these works should be thoroughly read of a child in this time, which were almost impossible. But I only desire that they have in every of the said books so much instruction that they may take thereby some profit. Then the child's courage,[18] inflamed by the frequent reading of noble poets, daily more and more desireth to have experience in those things that they so vehemently do commend in them that they write of.

Leonidas, the noble king of Spartans, being once demanded of what estimation in poetry Tyrtaeus (as he supposed) was, it is written that he answering said, that for stirring the minds of young men he was excellent, for as much as they being moved with his verses do run into the battle, regarding no peril, as men all inflamed in martial courage. And when a man is come to mature years, and that reason in him is confirmed with serious learning and long experience, then shall he in reading tragedies execrate and abhor the intolerable life of tyrants; and shall contemn the folly and dotage expressed by poets lascivious.

Here will I leave to speak of the first part of a nobleman's study. And now will I write of the second part, which is more serious, and containeth in it sundry manners of learning.

[17] seizes   [18] spirit

11

The Most Commodious and Necessary
Studies Succeeding Ordinately[1]
the Lesson of Poets

After that fourteen years be passed of a child's age, his master, if he can, or some other studiously exercised in the art of an orator shall first read to him somewhat of that part of logic that is called *topica,* either of Cicero or else of that noble clerk[2] of Almaine[3] which late flowered, called [Rudolf] Agricola, whose work prepareth invention, telling the places from whence an argument for the proof of any matter may be taken with little study. And that lesson with much and diligent learning, having mixed therewith none other exercise, will in the space of half a year be perfectly conned.

Immediately after that, the art of rhetoric would be semblably[4] taught, either in Greek out of Hermogenes, or of Quintilian in Latin, beginning at the third book and instructing diligently the child in that part of rhetoric principally which concerneth persuasion, for as much as it is most apt for consultations. There can be no shorter instruction of rhetoric than the treatise that Tully[5] wrote unto his son, which book is named the *Partition of Rhetoric.*

[1] In order   [2] scholar
[3] Germany   [4] similarly
[5] Cicero

And in good faith, to speak boldly that I think: for him that needeth not or doth not desire to be an exquisite orator, the little book made by the famous Erasmus (whom all gentle wits are bound to thank and support) which he calleth *Copiam verborum et rerum,* that is to say, "Plenty of Words and Matters," shall be sufficient.

Isocrates concerning the lesson of orators is every where wonderful profitable, having almost as many wise sentences[6] as he hath words; and with that is so sweet and delectable to read that after him almost all other seem unsavory and tedious; and in persuading as well a prince as a private person to virtue, in two very little and compendious works, whereof he made the one to King Nicocles, the other to his friend Demonicus, would be perfectly conned and had in continual memory.

Demosthenes and Tully, by the consent of all learned men, have pre-eminence and sovereignty over all orators, the one reigning in wonderful eloquence in the public weal of the Romans, who had the empire and dominion of all the world, the other of no less estimation in the city of Athens, which of long time was accounted the mother of sapience and the palace of muses and all liberal sciences. Of which two orators may be attained not only eloquence excellent and perfect, but also precepts of wisdom and gentle manners, with most commodious examples of all noble virtues and policy. Wherefore the master in reading them must well observe and express the parts and colors of rhetoric in them contained, according to the precepts of that art before learned.

The utility that a nobleman shall have by reading these orators is that when he shall happen to reason in council, or shall speak in a great audience, or to strange ambassadors of great princes, he shall not be constrained

---

[6] thoughts

to speak words sudden and disordered, but shall bestow them aptly and in their places. Wherefore the most noble emperor Octavius is highly commended, for that he never spoke in the Senate or to the people of Rome but in an oration prepared and purposely made.

Also to prepare the child to understanding of histories, which, being replenished with the names of countries and towns unknown to the reader do make the history tedious, or else the less pleasant—so if they be in any wise known, it increaseth an inexplicable delectation—it shall be therefore, and also for refreshing the wit, a convenient lesson to behold the old tables[7] of Ptolemy, wherein all the world is painted, having first some introduction into the sphere, whereof now of late be made very good treatises, and more plain and easy to learn than was wont to be. Albeit there is none so good learning as the demonstration of cosmography by material figures and instruments, having a good instructor. And surely this lesson is both pleasant and necessary. For what pleasure is it in one hour to behold those realms, cities, seas, rivers, and mountains that uneth[8] in an old man's life cannot be journeyed and pursued! What incredible delight is taken in beholding the diversities of people, beasts, fowls, fishes, trees, fruits, and herbs; to know the sundry manners and conditions of people, and the variety of their natures, and that in a warm study or parlor, without peril of the sea or danger of long and painful journeys! I cannot tell what more pleasure should happen to a gentle wit than to behold in his own house everything that within all the world is contained. The commodity thereof knew the great king Alexander, as some writers do remember. For he caused the countries, whereunto he purposed any enter-

[7] maps   [8] hardly

prise, diligently and cunningly to be described and
painted, that beholding the picture, he might perceive
which places were most dangerous, and where he and his
host might have most easy and covenable[9] passage. Semblably did the Romans in the rebellion of France and
the insurrection of their confederates, setting up a table
openly, wherein Italy was painted, to the intent that the
people looking in it should reason and consult in which
places it were best to resist or invade their enemies.

I omit, for length of the matter, to write of Cyrus the
great king of Persia, Crassus the Roman, and divers other
valiant and expert captains which have lost themselves
and all their army by ignorance of this doctrine. Wherefore it may not be of any wise man denied but that cosmography is to all noblemen not only pleasant but profitable also, and wonderful necessary.

In the part of cosmography wherewith history is min-
gled, Strabo reigneth, which took his argument of the
divine poet Homer. Also Strabo himself (as he saith)
labored a great part of Africa and Egypt, where undoubtedly be many things to be marveled at.

Solinus writeth almost in like form, and is more brief,
and hath much more variety of things and matters, and
is therefore marvelous delectable; yet Mela is much
shorter, and his style (by reason that it is of a more antiquity) is also more clean and facile.[10] Wherefore he or
Dionysius shall be sufficient.

Cosmography being substantially perceived, it is then
time to induce a child to the reading of histories—but
first, to set him in a fervent courage,[11] the master in the
most pleasant and elegant wise expressing what incomparable delectation, utility, and commodity shall hap-

[9] suitable   [10] easy to understand
[11] spirit

pen to emperors, kings, princes, and all other gentlemen
by reading of histories, showing to him that Demetrius
Phalareus, a man of excellent wisdom and learning, and
which in Athens had been long exercised in the public
weal, exhorted Ptolemy King of Egypt chiefly above all
other studies to haunt and embrace histories and such
other books wherein were contained precepts made to
kings and princes, saying that in them he should read
those things which no man durst report unto his person.
Also Cicero, father of the Latin eloquence, calleth an
history the witness of times, mistress of life, the life of
remembrance, of truth the light, and messenger of antiquity. Moreover the sweet Isocrates exhorteth the king
Nicocles, whom he instructeth, to leave behind him
statues and images that shall represent rather the figure
and similitude of his mind than the features of his body,
signifying thereby the remembrance of his acts written
in histories.

By semblable advertisements[12] shall a noble heart be
trained to delight in histories. And then, according to
the counsel of Quintilian, it is best that he begin with
Titus Livius, not only for his elegancy of writing, which
floweth in him like a fountain of sweet milk, but also for
as much as by reading that author he may know how the
most noble city of Rome, of a small and poor beginning,
by prowess and virtue, little and little came to the empire
and dominion of all the world.

Also in that city he may behold the form of a public
weal, which if the insolency and pride of Tarquin had
not excluded kings out of the city, it had been the most
noble and perfect of all other.

Xenophon, being both a philosopher and an excellent
captain, so invented and ordered his work named *Paedia*

[12] admonitions

Cyri[13] (which may be interpreted the "Childhood or Discipline of Cyrus") that he leaveth to the readers thereof an incomparable sweetness and example of living, specially for the conducting and well ordering of hosts or armies. And therefore the noble Scipio, who was called Africanus, as well in peace as in war was never seen without this book of Xenophon.

With him may be joined Quintus Curtius, who writeth the life of King Alexander elegantly and sweetly. In whom may be found the figure of an excellent prince, as he that incomparably excelled all other kings and emperors in wisdom, hardiness, strength, policy, agility, valiant courage, nobility, liberality, and courtesy. Wherein he was a spectacle or mark for all princes to look on. Contrariwise, when he was once vanquished with voluptie[14] and pride, his tyranny and beastly cruelty abhorreth all readers. The comparison of the virtues of these two noble princes, equally described by two excellent writers well expressed, shall provoke a gentle courage to contend to follow their virtues.

Julius Caesar and Sallust, for their compendious writing, to the understanding whereof is required an exact and perfect judgment, and also for the exquisite order of battle, and continuing of the history without any variety, whereby the pain of study should be alleviate—they two would be reserved until he that shall read them shall see some experience in semblable matters. And then shall he find in them such pleasure and commodity as therewith a noble and gentle heart ought to be satisfied. For in them both it shall seem to a man that he is present and heareth the counsels and exhortations of captains, which be called *conciones,* and that he seeth the order of hosts when they be embattled, the fierce assaults and

[13] *Cyropaedia*   [14] voluptuousness

encounterings of both armies, the furious rage of that
monster called war. And he shall wene[15] that he heareth
the terrible dints of sundry weapons and ordnance of
battle, the conduct and policies of wise and expert captains—specially in the commentaries of Julius Caesar
which he made of his exploiture[16] in France and Britain,
and other countries now reckoned among the provinces
of Germany. Which book is studiously to be read of the
princes of this realm of England and their counselors,
considering that thereof may be taken necessary instructions concerning the wars against Irishmen or Scots, who
be of the same rudeness and wild disposition that the
Swiss and Britons were in the time of Caesar. Semblable
utility shall be found in the history of Titus Livius in
his third decades,[17] where he writeth of the battles that
the Romans had with Hannibal and the Carthaginians.

Also there be divers orations, as well in all the books
of the said authors as in the history of Cornelius Tacitus,
which be very delectable, and for counsels very expedient
to be had in memory. And in good faith I have often
thought that the consultations and orations written by
Tacitus do import a majesty with a compendious eloquence therein contained.

In the learning of these authors, a young gentleman
shall be taught to note and mark not only the order and
elegancy in declaration of the history, but also the occasion of the wars, the counsels and preparations on either
part, the estimation of the captains, the manner and
form of their governance, the continuance of the battle,
the fortune and success of the whole affairs. Semblably
out of the wars, in other daily affairs, the estate of the
public weal: if it be prosperous or in decay, what is the

very occasion of the one or of the other, the form and
manner of the governance thereof, the good and evil
qualities of them that be rulers, the commodities and
good sequel of virtue, the discommodities and evil conclusion of vicious license.

Surely if a nobleman do thus seriously and diligently
read histories, I dare affirm there is no study or science
for him of equal commodity and pleasure, having regard
to every time and age.

By the time that the child do come to seventeen years
of age, to the intent his courage be bridled with reason, it
were needful to read unto him some works of philosophy:
specially that part that may inform him unto virtuous
manners, which part of philosophy is called moral.
Wherefore there would be read to him for an introduction two the first books[18] of the work of Aristotle called
Ethicae, wherein is contained the definitions and proper
significations of every virtue; and that to be learned in
Greek, for the translations that we yet have, be but a
rude and gross shadow of the eloquence and wisdom of
Aristotle.   Forthwith would follow the work of Cicero
called in Latin *De officiis,* whereunto yet is no proper
English word to be given; but to provide for it some
manner of exposition, it may be said in this form: "Of
the Duties and Manners Appertaining to Men."   But
above all other, the works of Plato would be most studiously read, when the judgment of a man is come to perfection, and by the other studies is instructed in the form
of speaking that philosophers used.   Lord God, what incomparable sweetness of words and matter shall he find
in the said works of Plato and Cicero!   Wherein is joined
gravity with delectation, excellent wisdom with divine
eloquence, absolute virtue with pleasure incredible; and

[18] that is, the first two books

every place is so infarced[19] with profitable counsel, joined with honesty, that those three books be almost sufficient to make a perfect and excellent governor.

The proverbs of Solomon, with the books of Ecclesiastes and Ecclesiasticus, be very good lessons. All the historical parts of the Bible be right necessary for to be read of a nobleman, after that he is mature in years. And the residue (with the New Testament) is to be reverently touched, as a celestial jewel or relic, having the chief interpreter of those books true and constant faith, and dreadfully to set hands thereon—remembering that Uzzah for putting his hand to the holy shrine (that was called *Archa federis*) when it was brought by King David from the city of Gibeah, though it were wavering and in danger to fall, yet was he stricken of God, and fell dead immediately. It would not be forgotten that the little book of the most excellent doctor Erasmus Roterodamus (which he wrote to Charles, now being emperor, and then Prince of Castile), which book is entitled the *Institution of a Christian Prince,* would be as familiar alway with gentlemen at all times and in every age as was Homer with the great king Alexander, or Xenophon with Scipio. For as all men may judge that have read that work of Erasmus, that there was never book written in Latin that, in so little a portion, contained of sentence, eloquence, and virtuous exhortation a more compendious abundance.

And here I make an end of the learning and study whereby noblemen may attain to be worthy to have authority in a public weal. Alway I shall exhort tutors and governors of noble children that they suffer them not to use ingourgitations[20] of meat or drink, ne[21] to sleep much, that is to say, above eight hours at the most. For

[19] stuffed

[20] guzzlings or swillings

[21] nor

undoubtedly both repletion and superfluous sleep be capital enemies to study, as they be semblably to health of body and soul. Aulus Gellius saith that children, if they use of meat and sleep overmuch, be made therewith dull to learn; and we see that thereof slowness is taken, and the children's personages do wax uncomely, and less grow in stature. Galen will not permit that pure wine, without allay[22] of water, should in any wise be given to children, for as much as it humecteth[23] the body or maketh it moister and hotter than is convenient; also it filleth the head with fume,[24] in them specially which be like as children of hot and moist temperature. These be well nigh the words of the noble Galen.

[22] alloy, mixture   [23] moistens
[24] vapor

12

Why Gentlemen in This Present Time Be Not Equal in Doctrine[1] to the Ancient Noblemen

Now will I somewhat declare of the chief causes why in our time noblemen be not as excellent in learning as they were in old time among the Romans and Greeks. Surely as I have diligently marked in daily experience, the principal causes be these: the pride, avarice, and negligence of parents, and the lack or fewness of sufficient masters or teachers.

As I said, pride is the first cause of this inconvenience. For of those persons be some which without shame dare affirm that, to a great gentleman, it is a notable reproach to be well learned, and to be called a great clerk;[2] which name they account to be of so base estimation that they never have it in their mouths but when they speak anything in derision; which perchance they would not do if they had once leisure to read our own chronicle of England, where they shall find that King Henry the First, son of William [the] Conqueror, and one of the most noble princes that ever reigned in this realm, was openly called Henry beau clerke: which is in English, "fair clerk," and is yet at this day so named. And whether that name be to his honor or to his reproach, let them

---

[1] Learning   [2] scholar

judge that do read and compare his life with his two
brethren, William, called Rouse,[3] and Robert le Courtoise, they both not having semblable[4] learning with the
said Henry; the one for his dissolute living and tyranny
being hated of all his nobles and people, finally was suddenly slain by the shot of an arrow as he was hunting in
a forest, which, to make larger, and to give his deer more
liberty, he did cause the houses of his parishes to be
pulled down, the people to be expelled, and all being
desolate, to be turned into desert, and made only pasture
for beasts savage. Which he would never have done if he
had as much delighted in good learning as did his
brother. The other brother, Robert le Courtoise, being
Duke of Normandy and the eldest son of William [the]
Conqueror, albeit that he was a man of much prowess
and right expert in martial affairs (wherefore he was
elect before Godfrey of Boulogne to have been king of
Jerusalem), yet notwithstanding, when he invaded this
realm with sundry puissant armies, also divers noblemen
aiding him, yet his noble brother Henry beau clerke, more
by wisdom than power, also by learning, adding policy
to virtue and courage, oftentimes vanquished him and did
put him to flight. And after sundry victories, finally
took him and kept him in prison, having none other
means to keep his realm in tranquillity.

It was for no rebuke, but for an excellent honor, that
the emperor Antonine was surnamed philosopher, for
his most noble example of living and industry incomparable; he during all the time of his reign kept the public weal of the Romans in such a perfect estate that by
his acts he confirmed the saying of Plato, that "Blessed
is that public weal wherein either philosophers do reign,

---

[3] William Rufus (William II of England, $r.$ 1087–1100)
[4] similar

or else kings be in philosophy studious." These persons that so much contemn learning that they would that gentlemen's children should have no part or very little thereof, but rather should spend their youth alway (I say not only in hunting and hawking, which, moderately used, as solaces ought to be, I intend not to dispraise) but in those idle pastimes which, for the vice that is therein, the commandment of the prince and the universal consent of the people expressed in statutes and laws do prohibit—I mean playing at dice and other games named unlawful—these persons, I say, I would should remember, or else now learn if they never else heard it, that the noble Philip, King of Macedonia, who subdued all Greece, above all the good fortunes that ever he had, most rejoiced that his son Alexander was born in the time that Aristotle the philosopher flourished, by whose instruction he might attain to most excellent learning. Also the same Alexander oftentimes said that he was equally as much bound to Aristotle as to his father King Philip: for of his father he received life, but of Aristotle he received the way to live nobly.

Who dispraised Epaminondas, the most valiant captain of Thebans, for that he was excellently learned and a great philosopher? Who ever discommended Julius Caesar for that he was a noble orator, and next to Tully[5] in the eloquence of the Latin tongue excelled all other? Who ever reproved the emperor Hadrian for that he was so exquisitely learned, not only in Greek and Latin but also in all sciences liberal, that openly at Athens in the universal assembly of the greatest clerks of the world, he by a long time disputed with philosophers and rhetoricians which were esteemed most excellent, and by the judgment of them that were present had the palm or re-

[5] Cicero

ward of victory? And yet by the governance of that noble
emperor, not only the public weal flourished, but also
divers rebellions were suppressed, and the majesty of the
empire hugely increased. Was it any reproach to the
noble Germanicus (who by the assignment of Augustus
should have succeeded Tiberius in the empire, if traitor-
ous envy had not in his flourishing youth bereft him his
life) that he was equal to the most noble poets of his
time, and to the increase of his honor and most worthy
commendation, his image was set up at Rome in the habit
that poets at those days used?

Finally how much excellent learning commendeth and
not dispraiseth nobility, it shall plainly appear unto them
that do read the lives of Alexander, called Severus,
Tacitus, Probus, Aurelius, Constantine, Theodosius, and
Charles the Great, surnamed Charlemagne, all being
emperors, and do compare them with other which lacked
or had not so much of doctrine. Verily they be far from
good reason, in mine opinion, which covet to have their
children goodly in stature, strong, deliver,[6] well singing
—wherein trees, beasts, fishes, and birds be not only with
them equal, but also far do exceed them—and cunning,[7]
whereby only man excelleth all other creatures in earth,
they reject and account unworthy to be in their children.
What unkind[8] appetite[9] were it to desire to be father
rather of a piece of flesh, that can only move and feel,
than of a child that should have the perfect form of a
man? What so perfectly expresseth a man as doctrine?
Diogenes the philosopher, seeing one without learning
sit on a stone, said to them that were with him, "Behold
where one stone sitteth on another." Which words, well

6 nimble   7 knowledge, intelligence
8 strange, injurious   9 inclination

considered and tried, shall appear to contain in it wonderful matter for the approbation of doctrine. Whereof a wise man may accumulate inevitable arguments: which I of necessity, to avoid tediousness, must needs pass over at this time.

13

The Second and Third Decay of Learning Among Gentlemen

The second occasion wherefore gentlemen's children seldom have sufficient learning is avarice: for where their parents will not adventure to send them far out of their proper countries—partly for fear of death, which perchance dare not approach them at home with their father, partly for expense of money, which they suppose would be less in their own houses, or in a village with some of their tenants or friends—having seldom any regard to the teacher, whether he be well learned or ignorant. For if they hire a schoolmaster to teach in their houses, they chiefly inquire with how small a salary he will be contented, and never do ensearch how much good learning he hath, and how among well learned men he is therein esteemed—using therein less diligence than in taking servants, whose service is of much less importance, and to a good schoolmaster is not in profit to be compared. A gentleman, ere he take a cook into his service, he will first diligently examine him, how many sorts of meats, potages, and sauces he can perfectly make, and how well he can season them, that they may be both pleasant and nourishing. Yea and if it be but a falconer, he will scrupulously inquire what skill he hath in feeding, called diet, and keeping of his hawk from all sickness; also how he can reclaim her and prepare her to flight. And to such a cook or falconer, whom he findeth expert, he spareth not to give much wages with other bounteous rewards. But of a schoolmaster, to whom he will commit his child to be fed with learning and instructed in virtue, whose life shall be the principal monument of his name and honor, he never maketh further inquiry but where he may have a schoolmaster, and with how little charge; and if one be perchance found well learned, but he will not take pains to teach without he may have a great salary, he then speaketh nothing more, or else saith: "What, shall so much wages be given to a schoolmaster which would keep me two servants?" To whom may be said these words, that by his son being well learned he shall receive more commodity and also worship than by the service of a hundred cooks and falconers.

The third cause of this hindrance is negligence of parents, which I do specially note in this point: there have been divers as well gentlemen as of the nobility that, delighting to have their sons excellent in learning, have provided for them cunning masters, who substantially have taught them grammar, and very well instructed them to speak Latin elegantly, whereof the parents have taken much delectation; but when they have had of grammar sufficient and be come to the age of fourteen years, and do approach or draw toward the estate of man—which age is called mature or ripe (wherein not only the said learning continued by much experience shall be perfectly digested and confirmed in perpetual remembrance, but also more serious learning contained in other liberal sciences, and also philosophy would then be learned)—the parents, that thing nothing regarding, but being sufficed[1] that their children can only speak Latin properly or make verses without matter or

[1] satisfied

sentence,[2] they from thenceforth do suffer them to live in
idleness, or else, putting them to service, do as it were
banish them from all virtuous study or exercise of that
which they before learned. So that we may behold divers
young gentlemen who, in their infancy and childhood,
were wondered at for their aptness to learning, and
prompt speaking of elegant Latin, which, now being men,
not only have forgotten their congruity[3] (as is the common word) and unneth[4] can speak one whole sentence in
true Latin, but, that worse is, hath all learning in derision, and in scorn thereof will of wantonness speak the
most barbarously that they can imagine.

Now some man will require me to show mine opinion,
if it be necessary that gentlemen should after the age of
fourteen years continue in study. And to be plain and
true therein: I dare affirm that if the elegant speaking of
Latin be not added to other doctrine,[5] little fruit may
come of the tongue, since Latin is but a natural speech,
and the fruit of speech is wise sentence, which is gathered
and made of sundry learnings. And who that hath nothing but language only, may be no more praised than a
popinjay,[6] a pie,[7] or a stare[8] when they speak featly.[9]
There be many nowadays in famous schools and universities which be so much given to the study of tongues
only, that when they write epistles, they seem to the
reader that, like to a trumpet, they make a sound without
any purpose, whereunto men do harken more for the
noise than for any delectation that thereby is moved.
Wherefore they be much abused that suppose eloquence

[2] thought   [3] grammatical correctness
[4] scarcely   [5] learning
[6] parrot   [7] magpie
[8] starling   [9] cleverly

to be only in words or colors of rhetoric, for as Tully[10]
saith, what is so furious or mad a thing as a vain sound
of words of the best sort and most ornate, containing
neither cunning[11] nor sentence? Undoubtedly very[12] eloquence is in every tongue where any matter or act done
or to be done is expressed in words clean, propise,[13] ornate, and comely; whereof sentences be so aptly compact
that they by a virtue inexplicable do draw unto them the
minds and consent of the hearers, they being therewith
either persuaded, moved, or to delectation induced.

Also every man is not an orator that can write an
epistle or a flattering oration in Latin, whereof the last
(as God help me) is too much used. For a right orator
may not be without a much better furniture, Tully saying that to him belongeth the explicating or unfolding
of sentence with a great estimation, in giving counsel concerning matters of great importance; also to him appertaineth the stirring and quickening of people languishing
or despairing, and to moderate them that be rash and un-
bridled. Wherefore noble authors do affirm that in the
first infancy of the world, men wandering like beasts in
woods and on mountains, regarding neither the religion
due unto God nor the office[14] pertaining unto man, ordered all thing by bodily strength, until Mercurius (as
Plato supposeth), or some other man helped by sapience
and eloquence, by some apt or proper oration assembled
them together, and persuaded to them what commodity
was in mutual conversation and honest manners.

But yet Cornelius Tacitus describeth an orator to be
of more excellent qualities, saying that an orator is he

---

[10] Cicero
[11] knowledge, intelligence
[12] true, real
[13] suitable
[14] duty

that can or may speak or reason in every question sufficiently, elegantly; and to persuade properly, according
to the dignity of the thing that is spoken of, the opportunity of time, and pleasure of them that be hearers.
Tully before him affirmed that a man may not be an
orator heaped with praise but if he have gotten the
knowledge of all things and arts of greatest importance.
And how shall an orator speak of that thing that he hath
not learned? And because there may be nothing but it
may happen to come in praise or dispraise, in consultation or judgment, in accusation or defense, therefore an
orator by others' instruction perfectly furnished may in
every matter and learning commend or dispraise, exhort
or dissuade, accuse or defend eloquently, as occasion happeneth. Wherefore inasmuch as in an orator is required
to be a heap of all manner of learning—which of some is
called the world of science, of other the circle of doctrine,
which is in one word of Greek *encyclopedia*—therefore
at this day may be found but a very few orators. For they
that come in message from princes be for honor named
now orators if they be in any degree of worship, only
poor men having equal or more of learning being called
messengers. Also they which do only teach rhetoric—
which is the science whereby is taught an artificial form
of speaking wherein is the power to persuade, move, and
delight—or by that science only do speak or write without any adminiculation[15] of other sciences ought to
be named rhetoricians, declamators, artificial speakers
(named in Greek *logodedali*), or any other name than
orators.

Semblably[16] they that make verses expressing thereby
none other learning but the craft of versifying be not of

---

[15] support   [16] Likewise

ancient writers named poets, but only called versifiers.
For the name of a poet, whereat now (specially in this
realm) men have such indignation that they use only
poets and poetry in the contempt of eloquence, was in
ancient time in high estimation, in so much that all wisdom was supposed to be therein included, and poetry was
the first philosophy that ever was known. Whereby men
from their childhood were brought to the reason how to
live well, learning thereby not only manners and natural
affections, but also the wonderful works of nature, mix-
ing serious matter with things that were pleasant—as it
shall be manifest to them that shall be so fortunate to
read the noble works of Plato and Aristotle, wherein he
shall find the authority of poets frequently alleged. Yea,
and that more is: in poets was supposed to be science
mystical and inspired; and therefore in Latin they were
called *vates,* which word signifieth as much as prophets.
And therefore Tully in his *Tusculan Questions* supposeth
that a poet cannot abundantly express verses sufficient
and complete, or that his eloquence may flow without
labor words well sounding and plenteous, without celestial instinction.[17] Which is also by Plato ratified.

But since we be now occupied in the defense of poets,
it shall not be incongruent[18] to our matter to show what
profit may be taken by the diligent reading of ancient
poets, contrary to the false opinion that now reigneth of
them that suppose that in the works of poets is contained
nothing but bawdry (such is their foul word of reproach)
and unprofitable leasings.[19] But first I will interpret
some verses of Horace, wherein he expresseth the office
of poets; and after will I resort to a more plain demon-

[17] inspiration
[18] unsuitable
[19] lies

stration of some wisdoms and counsels contained in some verses of poets. Horace in his second book of *Epistles* saith in this wise, or much like:

> The poet fashioneth by some pleasant mean
> The speech of children tender and unsure,
> Pulling their ears from words unclean,
> Giving to them precepts that are pure,
> Rebuking envy and wrath if it dure.[20]
> Things well done he can by example commend.
> The needy and sick he doth also his cure
> To recomfort, if aught he can amend.

But they which be ignorant in poets will perchance object, as is their manner, against these verses, saying that in Terence and other that were writers of comedies —also Ovid, Catullus, Martial, and all that rout of lascivious poets that wrote epistles and ditties of love, some called in Latin *elegiae* and some *epigrammata*—is nothing contained but incitation to lechery. First, comedies, which they suppose to be a doctrinal of ribaldry, they be undoubtedly a picture or as it were a mirror of man's life. Wherein evil is not taught but discovered, to the intent that men beholding the promptness of youth unto vice, the snares of harlots and bawds laid for young minds, the deceit of servants, the chances of fortune contrary to men's expectation—they being thereof warned—may prepare themself to resist or prevent occasion. Semblably remembering the wisdoms, advertisements,[21] counsels, dissuasion from vice, and other profitable sentences most eloquently and familiarly showed in those comedies, undoubtedly there shall be no little fruit out of them gathered. And if the vices in them expressed should be cause

---

[20] lasts, endures   [21] admonitions

that minds of the readers should be corrupted, then by
the same argument not only interludes in English, but
also sermons wherein some vice is declared should be to
the beholders and hearers like occasion to increase sinners. And that by comedies good counsel is ministered, it
appeareth by the sentence of Parmeno in the second
comedy of Terence.

> In this thing I triumph in mine own conceit,
> That I have founden for all young men the way
> How they of harlots shall know the deceit—
> Their wits, their manners—that thereby they may
> Them perpetually hate. For so much as they
> Out of their own houses be fresh and delicate,
> Feeding curiously; at home all the day
> Living beggarly, in most wretched estate.

There be many more words spoken which I purposely
omit to translate, notwithstanding the substance of the
whole sentence is herein comprised.

But now to come to other poets, what may be better
said than is written by Plautus in his first comedy?

> Verily virtue doth all things excel.
> For if liberty, health, living, and substance,
> Our country, our parents and children do well,
> It happeneth by virtue: she doth all advance.
> Virtue hath all thing under governance.
> And in whom of virtue is founden great plenty,
> Anything that is good may never be dainty.[22]

Also Ovid, that seemeth to be most of all poets lascivious, in his most wanton books hath right commend-

---

[22] distasteful or unsavory to a true palate (?)

able and noble sentences, as for proof thereof I will recite some that I have taken at adventure:[23]

> Time is in medicine if it shall profit.
> Wine given out of time may be annoyance.
> A man shall irritate vice if he prohibit
> When time is not meet[24] unto his utterance.
> Therefore, if thou yet by counsel art recuperable.
> Flee thou from idleness, and alway be stable.

Martial, which for his dissolute writing is most seldom
read of men of much gravity, hath notwithstanding many
commendable sentences and right wise counsels, as
among divers I will rehearse one which is first come to
my remembrance:

> If thou wilt eschew bitter adventure,
> And avoid the gnawing of a pensiful[25] heart,
> Set in no one person all wholly thy pleasure:
> The less joy shalt thou have, but the less shalt
>   thou smart.

I could recite a great number of semblable good sentences out of these and other wanton poets, who in the
Latin do express them incomparably with more grace and
delectation to the reader than our English tongue may
yet comprehend. Wherefore since good and wise matter
may be picked out of these poets, it were no reason, for
some light matter that is in their verses, to abandon
therefore all their works, no more than it were to forbear
or prohibit a man to come into a fair garden lest the
redolent savors of sweet herbs and flowers shall move
him to wanton courage,[26] or lest in gathering good and

[23] at random

[24] propitious (?)

[25] pensive, sad

[26] appetite

wholesome herbs he may happen to be stung with a nettle. No wise man entereth into a garden but he soon espieth good herbs from nettles, and treadeth the nettles under his feet whiles he gathereth good herbs. Whereby he taketh no damage; or if he be stung, he maketh light of it, and shortly forgetteth it. Semblably if he do read wanton matter mixed with wisdom, he putteth the worst under foot, and sorteth out the best; or if his courage be stirred or provoked, he remembereth the little pleasure and great detriment that should ensue of it, and, withdrawing his mind to some other study or exercise, shortly forgetteth it. And therefore among the Jews, though it were prohibited to children until they came to ripe years to read the books of Genesis, of the Judges, *Cantica canticorum,* and some part of the book of Ezekiel the prophet—for that in them was contained some matter which might happen to incense the young mind, wherein were sparks of carnal concupiscence—yet after certain years of men's ages, it was lawful for every man to read and diligently study those works. So although I do not approve the lesson of wanton poets to be taught unto all children, yet think I convenient and necessary that, when the mind is become constant, and courage is assuaged, or that children of their natural disposition be shamefaced and continent, none ancient poet would be excluded from the lesson of such one as desireth to come to the perfection of wisdom.

But in defending of orators and poets, I had almost forgotten where I was. Verily there may no man be an excellent poet nor orator unless he have part of all other doctrine, specially of noble philosophy. And to say the truth, no man can apprehend the very delectation that is in the lesson of noble poets unless he have read very

much and in divers authors of divers learnings. Wherefore as I late said, to the augmentation of understanding,
called in Latin *intellectus et mens,* is required to be much
reading and vigilant study in every science, specially of
that part of philosophy named moral, which instructeth
men in virtue and politic governance. Also no noble author, specially of them that wrote in Greek or Latin before twelve hundred years past, is not for any cause to be
omitted. For therein I am of Quintilian's opinion, that
there is few or none ancient work that yieldeth not some
fruit or commodity to the diligent readers. And it is a
very gross or obstinate wit that, by reading much, is not
somewhat amended. Concerning the election of other
authors to be read, I have (as I trust) declared sufficiently
my conceit[27] and opinion in the tenth and eleventh chapters of this little treatise.

Finally, like as a delicate tree that cometh of a kernel,
which, as soon as it burgeoneth out leaves, if it be plucked
up or[28] it be sufficiently rooted, and laid in a corner, it
becometh dry or rotten, and no fruit cometh of it; if it
be removed and set in another air or earth which is of
contrary qualities where it was before, it either semblably
dieth, or beareth no fruit, or else the fruit that cometh of
it loseth his verdure and taste, and finally his estimation[29]—so the pure and excellent learning whereof I
have spoken, though it be sown in a child never so timely,
and springeth and burgeoneth never so pleasantly, if before it take a deep root in the mind of the child, it be
laid aside, either by too much solace,[30] or continual attendance in service, or else is translated to another study
which is of a more gross or unpleasant quality, before it

[27] judgment   [28] ere, before
[29] worth   [30] recreation

be confirmed or established by often reading or diligent exercise, in conclusion it vanisheth and cometh to nothing. Wherefore let men reply as they list, but in mine opinion men be wonderfully deceived nowadays (I dare not say with the persuasion of avarice) that do put their children at the age of fourteen or fifteen years to the study of the laws of the realm of England. I will show to them reasonable causes why, if they will patiently hear me, informed partly by mine own experience.

14

How the Students in the Laws of This Realm May Take Excellent Commodity by the Lessons of Sundry Doctrines

It may not be denied but that all laws be founded on the deepest part of reason, and, as I suppose, no one law so much as our own; and the deeper men do investigate reason, the more difficile or hard must needs be the study. Also that reverend study is involved in so barbarous a language that it is not only void of all eloquence, but also, being separate from the exercise of our law only, it serveth to no commodity or necessary purpose, no man understanding it but they which have studied the laws.

Then children at fourteen or fifteen years old—in which time springeth courage,[1] set all in pleasure, and pleasure is in nothing that is not facile[2] or elegant—being brought to the most difficult and grave learning which hath nothing illecebrous[3] or delicate[4] to tickle their tender wits and allure them to study (unless it be lucre, which a gentle wit little esteemeth), the more part, vanquished with tediousness, either do abandon the laws and unawares to their friends do give them to gaming and other (as I might say) idle business, now called pastimes; or else if they be in any wise thereto constrained, they apprehending a piece thereof—as if they being long

[1] vigor
[2] easily accomplished
[3] alluring
[4] delightful

in a dark dungeon only did see by the light of a candle—
then if after twenty or thirty years' study they happen to
come among wise men, hearing matters commen[t]ed of
concerning a public weal or outward affairs between
princes, they no less be astonished than of[5] coming out
of a dark house at noonday they were suddenly stricken
in the eyes with a bright sunbeam.

But I speak not this in reproach of lawyers, for I know
divers of them which in consultation will make a right
vehement reason, and so do some other which hath
neither law nor other learning; yet the one and the other,
if they were furnished with excellent doctrine,[6] their reason should be the more substantial and certain. There be
some also which by their friends be coarted[7] to apply
the study of the law only, and for lack of plenteous ex-
hibition[8] be let[9] of their liberty, wherefore they cannot
resort unto pastime—these of all other be most cast away,
for, nature repugning,[10] they unneth[11] taste anything that
may be profitable, and also their courage[12] is so mortified
(which yet by solace[13] perchance might be made quick
or apt to some other study or laudable exercise) that they
live ever after out of all estimation.[14]

Wherefore Tully[15] saith, "We should so endeavor ourselves that we strive not with the universal nature of man,
but that being conserved, let us follow our own proper
natures, that though there be studies more grave and of
more importance, yet ought we to regard the studies
whereto we be by our own nature inclined." And that
this sentence is true, we have daily experience, in this

[5] if (?)
[6] learning
[7] constrained
[8] maintenance
[9] deprived
[10] resisting
[11] hardly
[12] spirit
[13] recreation
[14] esteem
[15] Cicero

realm specially. For how many men be there that, having their sons in childhood aptly disposed by nature
to paint, to carve, or grave,[16] to embroider, or do other
like things wherein is any art commendable concerning
invention, but that as soon as they espy it, they be therewith displeased, and forthwith bindeth them apprentices
to tailors, to weavers, to tuckers,[17] and sometime to cob-
blers? Which have been the inestimable loss of many
good wits, and have caused that in the said arts Englishmen be inferiors to all other people, and be constrained,
if we will have anything well painted, carved, or embroidered, to abandon our own countrymen and resort
unto strangers. But more of this shall I speak in the next
volume. But to resort unto lawyers. I think verily if
children were brought up as I have written, and continually were retained in the right study of very[18] philosophy
until they passed the age of twenty-one years, and then
set to the laws of this realm (being once brought to a
more certain and compendious study, and either in
English, Latin, or good French, written in a more clean
and elegant style), undoubtedly they should become men
of so excellent wisdom that throughout all the world
should be found in no common weal more noble counselors, our laws not only comprehending most excellent
reasons, but also being gathered and compact (as I might
say) of the pure meal or flour sifted out of the best laws
of all other countries—as somewhat I do intend to prove
evidently in the next volume, wherein I will render mine
office or duty to that honorable study whereby my father
was advanced to a judge, and also I myself have attained
no little commodity.[19]

I suppose divers men there be that will say that the

---

[16] engrave   [17] cloth-finishers
[18] true   [19] advantage

sweetness that is contained in eloquence and the multitude of doctrines should utterly withdraw the minds of young men from the more necessary study of the laws of this realm. To them will I make a brief answer, but true it shall be and I trust sufficient to wise men. In the great multitude of young men which alway will repair[20] —and the law being once brought into a more certain and perfect language, will also increase in the reverent study of the law—undoubtedly there shall never lack but some by nature inclined, divers by desire of sundry doctrines, many for hope of lucre or some other advancement, will effectually study the laws, ne[21] will be therefrom withdrawn by any other lesson which is more eloquent. Example we have at this present time of divers excellent learned men, both in the laws civil as also in physic,[22] which, being exactly studied in all parts of eloquence both in the Greek tongue and Latin, have notwithstanding read and perused the great fardels[23] and trusses[24] of the most barbarous authors stuffed with innumerable glosses—whereby the most necessary doctrines of law and physic be minced into fragments—and, in all wise men's opinions, do perceive no less in the said learnings than they which never knew eloquence, or never tasted other but the feces or dregs of the said noble doctrines. And as for the multitude of sciences cannot indamage any student, but if he be moved to study the law by any of the said motions by me before touched, he shall rather increase therein than be hindered; and that shall appear manifestly to them that either will give credence to my report or else will read the works that I will allege—which if they understand not, to desire some learned

[20] resort to (the study of law) [21] nor
[22] medicine [23] bundles
[24] packs

man by interpreting to cause them perceive it. And first I will begin at orators, who bear the principal title of eloquence.

It is to be remembered that in the learning of the laws of this realm, there is at this day an exercise wherein is a manner, a shadow, or figure of the ancient rhetoric. I mean the pleading used in court and Chancery called moots, where first a case is appointed to be mooted by certain young men containing some doubtful controversy, which is instead of the head of a declamation, called *thema*. The case being known, they which be appointed to moot, do examine the case, and investigate what they therein can espy which may make a contention, whereof may rise a question to be argued (and that of Tully is called *constitutio*, and of Quintilian *status causae*). Also they consider what pleas on every part ought to be made, and how the case may be reasoned: which is the first part of rhetoric, named *invention;* then appoint they how many pleas may be made for every part, and in what formality they should be set: which is the second part of rhetoric, called *disposition*. Wherein they do much approach unto rhetoric; then gather they all into perfect remembrance, in such order as it ought to be pleaded: which is the part of rhetoric named *memory*. But for as much as the tongue wherein it is spoken is barbarous, and the stirring of affections of the mind in this realm was never used, therefore there lacketh *elocution* and *pronunciation*, two the principal parts of rhetoric. Notwithstanding, some lawyers, if they be well retained,[25] will in a mean cause pronounce right vehemently. Moreover there seemeth to be, in the said pleadings, certain parts of an oration: that is to say, for *narrations, partitions, confirmations,* and *confutations* (named of some

[25] paid

reprehensions), they have *declarations, bars, replications,* and *rejoinders.* Only they lack pleasant form of beginning, called in Latin *exordium;* nor it maketh thereof no great matter—they that have studied rhetoric shall perceive what I mean. Also in arguing their cases, in mine opinion, they very little do lack of the whole art; for therein they do diligently observe the rules of confirmation and confutation, wherein resteth proof and disproof, having almost all the places whereof they shall fetch their reasons, called of orators *loci communes*—which I omit to name, fearing to be too long in this matter.

And verily I suppose, if there might once happen some man having an excellent wit to be brought up in such form as I have hitherto written, and may also be exactly or deeply learned in the art of an orator, and also in the laws of this realm, the prince so willing and thereto assisting, undoubtedly it should not be impossible for him to bring the pleading and reasoning of the law to the ancient form of noble orators. And the laws and exercise thereof, being in pure Latin or doulce[26] French, few men in consultations should (in mine opinion) compare with our lawyers, by this means being brought to be perfect orators, as in whom should then be found the sharp wits of logicians, the grave sentences of philosophers, the elegancy of poets, the memory of civilians,[27] the voice and gesture of them that can pronounce comedies—which is all that Tully, in the person of the most eloquent man Marcus Antonius, could require to be in an orator.

But now to conclude mine assertion, what let[28] was eloquence to the study of the law in Quintus Scaevola, which, being an excellent author in the laws civil, was called of all lawyers most eloquent? Or how much was

[26] pure
[27] students of the civil law
[28] hindrance

eloquence minished[29] by knowledge of the laws in Crassus, which was called of all eloquent men the best lawyer? Also Ser.vus Sulpitius, in his time one of the most noble orators next unto Tully, was not so let by eloquence but that on the civil laws he made notable comments, and many noble works, by all lawyers approved. Who readeth the text of civil [law], called the *Pandects* or *Digests,* and hath any commendable judgment in the Latin tongue, but he will affirm that Ulpian, Scaevola, Claudius, and all the other there named, of whose sayings all the said texts be assembled, were not only studious of eloquence but also wonderful exercised, for as much as their style doth approach nearer to the antique and pure eloquence than any other kind of writers that wrote about that time? Semblably[30] Tully, in whom it seemeth that eloquence hath set her glorious throne most richly and preciously adorned for all men to wonder at, but no man to approach it, was not let from being an incomparable orator, ne was not by the exact knowledge of other sciences withdrawn from pleading infinite causes before the Senate and judges, and they being of most weighty importance. In so much as Cornelius Tacitus, an excellent orator, historian, and lawyer, saith: "Surely in the books on Tully, men may deprehend[31] that in him lacked not the knowledge of geometry, ne music, ne grammar, finally of no manner of art that was honest; he of logic perceived the subtlety, of that part that was moral all the commodity, and of all things the chief motions and causes." And yet for all this abundance, and as it were a garner heaped with all manner sciences, there failed not in him substantial learning in the laws civil, as it may appear as well in the books which he him-

[29] diminished   [30] Likewise
[31] detect

self made of laws, as also, and most specially, in many of his most eloquent orations. Which if one well learned in the laws of this realm did read and well understand, he should find, specially in his orations called *Actions Against Verres,* many places where he should espy, by likelihood, the fountains from whence proceeded divers grounds of our common laws. But I will now leave to speak any more thereof at this time.

All that I have written well considered, it shall seem to wise men that neither eloquence nor knowledge of sundry doctrines shall utterly withdraw all men from study of the laws. But although many were allected[32] unto those doctrines by natural disposition, yet the same nature, which will not (as I might say) be circumscribed within the bounds of a certain of studies, may as well dispose some man as well to desire the knowledge of the laws of this realm as she did incline the Romans excellently learned in all sciences to apprehend the laws civil, since the laws of this realm, being well gathered and brought in good Latin, shall be worthy to have like praise as Tully gave to the laws comprehended in the twelve tables, from whence all civil law flowed. Which praise was in this wise (although men will abraid[33] at it, I will say as I think): the one little book of the twelve tables seemeth to me to surmount the libraries of all the philosophers in weighty authority and abundance of profit, behold who so will the fountains and heads of the laws.

Moreover, when young men have read laws expounded in the orations of Tully, and also in histories of the beginning of laws, and in the works of Plato, Xenophon, and Aristotle of the diversities of laws and public weals, if nature (as I late said) will dispose them to that manner

[32] enticed   [33] start

study, they shall be thereto the more incensed,[34] and come unto it the better prepared and furnished. And they whom nature thereto nothing moveth have not only saved all that time which many nowadays do consume in idleness, but also have won such a treasure whereby they shall alway be able to serve honorably their prince and the public weal of their country, principally if they confer all their doctrines to the most noble study of moral philosophy, which teacheth both virtues, manners, and civil policy. Whereby at the last we should have in this realm sufficiency of worshipful lawyers, and also a public weal equivalent to the Greeks or Romans.

[34] stirred up

15

For What Cause at This Day There Be in This Realm Few Perfect Schoolmasters

Lord God, how many good and clean wits of children be nowadays perished by ignorant schoolmasters! How little substantial doctrine[1] is apprehended by the fewness of good grammarians! Notwithstanding, I know that there be some well learned which have taught and also do teach; but God knoweth, a few, and they with small effect, having thereto no comfort, their aptest and most proper scholars, after they be well instructed in speaking Latin and understanding some poets, being taken from their school by their parents, and either be brought to the court and made lackeys or pages, or else are bound prentices; whereby the worship that the master, above any reward, coveteth to have by the praise of his scholar is utterly drowned. Whereof I have heard schoolmasters very well learned, of good right complain. But yet (as I said) the fewness of good grammarians is a great impediment of doctrine (and here I would the readers should mark that I note to be few good grammarians and not none). I call not them grammarians which only can teach or make rules whereby a child shall only learn to speak congrue[2] Latin, or to make six verses standing in one foot, wherein perchance shall be neither sentence[3] nor elo-

[1] learning   [2] grammatically correct
[3] thought

quence. But I name him a grammarian, by the authority of Quintilian, that, speaking Latin elegantly, can
expound good authors, expressing the invention and
disposition of the matter, their style or form of eloquence,
explicating the figures, as well of sentences as words,
leaving nothing, person or place named by the author, un-
declared or hid from his scholars. Wherefore Quintilian
saith: "It is not enough for him to have read poets, but
all kinds of writing must also be sought for: not for the
histories only, but also for the propriety of words, which
commonly do receive their authority of noble authors.
Moreover, without music, grammar may not be perfect,
for as much as therein must be spoken of meters and
harmonies, called *rythmi* in Greek. Neither if he have
not the knowledge of stars, he may understand poets,
which in description of times (I omit other things) they
treat of the rising and going down of planets. Also he
may not be ignorant in philosophy—for many places that
be almost in every poet, fetched out of the most subtle
part of natural questions." These be well nigh the words
of Quintilian. Then behold how few grammarians, after
this description, be in this realm.

Undoubtedly there be in this realm many well learned
which, if the name of a schoolmaster were not so much
had in contempt, and also if their labors with abundant
salaries might be requited, were right sufficient and able
to induce their hearers to excellent learning—so they be
not plucked away green, and ere they be in doctrine sufficiently rooted. But nowadays, if to a bachelor or master
of art study of philosophy waxeth tedious, if he have a
spoonful of Latin, he will show forth a hogshead without
any learning, and offer to teach grammar and expound
noble writers, and to be in the room of a master; he will
for a small salary set a false color of learning on proper

wits,[4] which will be washed away with one shower of
rain. For if the children be absent from school by the
space of one month, the best learned of them will unneth[5]
tell whether *Fato,* whereby Aeneas was brought into
Italy, were other[6] a man, a horse, a ship, or a wild goose—
although their master will perchance avaunt[7] himself to
be a good philosopher. Some men peradventure[8] do think
that at the beginning of learning it forceth[9] not although[10]
the masters have not so exact doctrine as I have rehearsed; but let them take good heed what Quintilian
saith, that "It is so much the better to be instructed by
them that are best learned, for as much as it is difficulty
to put out of the mind that which is once settled, the
double burden being painful to the masters that shall
succeed; and verily much more to unteach than to teach.
Wherefore it is written that Timothy, the noble musician,
demanded alway a greater reward of them whom other
had taught than of them that never anything learned."
These be the words of Quintilian or like.

Also common experience teacheth that no man will
put his son to a butcher to learn or[11] he bind him prentice
to a tailor; or if he will have him a cunning goldsmith,
will bind him first prentice to a tinker. In these things
poor men be circumspect, and the nobles and gentlemen,
who would have their sons by excellent learning come
unto honor, for sparing of cost, or for lack of diligent
search for a good schoolmaster, willfully destroy their
children, causing them to be taught that learning which
would require six or seven years to be forgotten. By
which time the more part of that age is spent wherein is

---

[4] minds   [5] scarcely
[6] either   [7] boast
[8] perhaps   [9] matters
[10] whether   [11] before

the chief sharpness of wit, called in Latin *acumen;* and also then approacheth the stubborn age, where the child brought up in pleasure disdaineth correction.

Now have I all declared (as I do suppose) the chief impeachments[12] of excellent learning. Of the reformation I need not to speak, since it is apparent that, by the contraries, men pursuing it earnestly with discreet judgment and liberality,[13] it would soon be amended.

[12] obstructions   [13] generosity

16

Of Sundry Forms of Exercise Necessary
for Every Gentleman

Although I have hitherto advanced the commendation of learning, specially in gentlemen, yet it is to be considered that continual study, without some manner of exercise, shortly exhausteth the spirits vital, and hindereth natural decoction[1] and digestion, whereby man's body is the sooner corrupted and brought into divers sicknesses, and finally the life is thereby made shorter. Where contrariwise by exercise, which is a vehement motion (as Galen prince of physicians defineth), the health of man is preserved, and his strength increased—for as much as the members, by moving and mutual touching, do wax more hard, and natural heat in all the body is thereby augmented. Moreover it maketh the spirits of a man more strong and valiant, so that, by the hardness of the members, all labors be more tolerable; by natural heat, the appetite is the more quick; the change of the substance received is the more ready; the nourishing of all parts of the body is the more sufficient and sure. By valiant motion of the spirits, all things superfluous be expelled, and the conduits of the body cleansed. Wherefore this part of physic[2] is not to be contemned or neglected in the education of children, and specially from the age of fourteen years upward, in which time strength with courage[3] increaseth.

[1] digesting in the stomach (regarded as a kind of cooking)
[2] medicine   [3] spirit

Moreover there be divers manners of exercises, whereof some only prepareth and helpeth digestion, some augmenteth also strength and hardness of body, other serveth for agility and nimbleness, some for celerity or speediness. There be also [some] which ought to be used for necessity only. All these ought he that is a tutor to a nobleman to have in remembrance, and, as opportunity serveth, to put them in experience. And specially them which with health do join commodity and (as I might say) necessity—considering that be he never so noble or valiant, sometime he is subject to peril, or (to speak it more pleasantly) servant to fortune.

Touching such exercises as many[4] be used within the house, or in the shadow (as is the old manner of speaking)—as deambulations,[5] laboring with poises made of lead or other metal (called in Latin *alteres*), lifting and throwing the heavy stone or bar, playing at tennis, and divers semblable[6] exercises—I will for this time pass over, exhorting them which do understand Latin, and do desire to know the commodities of sundry exercises, to resort to the book of Galen of the governance of health, called in Latin *De sanitate tuenda*, where they shall be in that matter abundantly satisfied, and find in the reading much delectation. Which book is translated into Latin wonderful eloquently by Doctor Linacre, late most worthy physician to our most noble sovereign lord, King Henry the VIII. And I will now only speak of those exercises apt to the furniture[7] of a gentleman's personage: adapting his body to hardness, strength, and agility, and to help therewith himself in peril, which may happen in wars or other necessity.

[4] may (?)	[5] walks
[6] similar	[7] equipping

17

Exercises Whereby Should Grow Both
Recreation and Profit

Wrestling is a very good exercise in the beginning of youth, so that it be with one that is equal in strength, or somewhat under, and that the place be soft, that in falling their bodies be not bruised. There be divers manners of wrestlings, but the best, as well for health of body as for exercise of strength, is when, laying mutually their hands one over another's neck, with the other hand they hold fast each other by the arm, and, clasping their legs together, they enforce themselves with strength and agility to throw down each other, which is also praised by Galen. And undoubtedly it shall be found profitable in wars, in case that a captain shall be constrained to cope with his adversary hand to hand, having his weapon broken or lost. Also it hath been seen that the weaker person, by the sleight of wrestling, hath overthrown the stronger, almost or[1] he could fasten on the other any violent stroke.

Also running is both a good exercise and a laudable solace. It is written of Epaminondas, the valiant captain of Thebans, who as well in virtue and prowess as in learning surmounted all noblemen of his time, that daily he exercised himself, in the morning with running and leaping, in the evening in wrestling, to the intent that likewise in armor he might the more strongly, embracing

---

[1] before

his adversary, put him in danger. And also that in the chase, running and leaping, he might either overtake his enemy or, being pursued, if extreme need required, escape him. Semblably[2] before him did the worthy Achilles, for whiles his ships lay at rode,[3] he suffered not his people to slumber in idleness, but daily exercised them and himself in running, wherein he was most excellent and passed all other; and therefore Homer, throughout all his work, calleth him swift-foot Achilles. The great Alexander, being a child, excelled all his companions in running. Wherefore, on a time, one demanded of him if he would run at the great game of Olympus, whereto out of all parts of Greece came the most active and valiant persons to assay masteries.[4] Whereunto Alexander answered in this form: "I would very gladly run there if I were sure to run with kings; for if I should contend with a private person, having respect to our both estates, our victories should not be equal." Needs must running be taken for a laudable exercise, since one of the most noble captains of all the Romans took his name of running, and was called *Papirius Cursor,* which is in English, Papirius the Runner. And also the valiant Marius the Roman, when he had been seven times consul, and was of the age of four score years, exercised himself daily among the young men of Rome in such wise that there resorted people out of far parts to behold the strength and agility of that old consul, wherein he compared with the young and lusty soldiers.

There is an exercise which is right profitable in extreme danger of wars; but because there seemeth to be some peril in the learning thereof, and also it hath not

---

[2] Likewise   [3] at anchor
[4] attempt victories

been of long time much used, specially among noblemen, perchance some readers will little esteem it—I mean swimming. But notwithstanding, if they revolve[5] the imbecility[6] of our nature, the hazards and dangers of battle —with the examples which shall hereafter be showed— they will (I doubt not) think it as necessary to a captain or man of arms as any that I have yet rehearsed. The Romans, who above all things had most in estimation martial prowess, they had a large and spacious field without the city of Rome which was called Mars' field, in Latin *Campus Martius,* wherein the youth of the city was exercised. This field adjoined to the river of Tiber, to the intent that as well men as children should wash and refresh them in the water after their labors, as also learn to swim. And not men and children only, but also the horses: that by such usage they should more aptly and boldly pass over great rivers, and be more able to resist or cut the waves, and not be afeared of pirries[7] or great storms. For it hath been oftentimes seen that by the good swimming of horses, many men have been saved, and contrariwise, by a timorous royle,[8] where the water hath unneth[9] come to his belly, his legs hath faltered; whereby many a good and proper man hath perished. What benefit received the whole city of Rome by the swimming of Horatius Cocles! Which is a noble history, and worthy to be remembered.

After the Romans had expelled Tarquin their king, as I have before remembered, he desired aid of Porsena, king of Tuscans, a noble and valiant prince, to recover eftsoons[10] his realm and dignity; who with a great and

---

[5] consider
[7] squalls
[9] hardly

[6] feebleness
[8] a Flemish horse (Croft's gloss)
[10] straightway

puissant[11] host besieged the city of Rome, and so suddenly and sharply assaulted it, that it lacked but little
that he ne had[12] entered into the city with his host over
the bridge called *Sublicius,* where encountered with him
this Horatius with a few Romans. And whiles this noble
captain, being alone, with an incredible strength resisted
all the host of Porsena that were on the bridge, he commanded the bridge to be broken behind him, wherewith
all the Tuscans thereon standing fell into the great river
of Tiber, but Horatius all armed lept into the water and
swam to his company, albeit that he was stricken with
many arrows and darts, and also grievously wounded.
Notwithstanding, by his noble courage and feat of swimming he saved the city of Rome from perpetual servitude,
which was likely to have ensued by the return of the
proud Tarquin.

How much profited the feat in swimming to the valiant Julius Caesar, who at the battle of Alexandria, on a
bridge being abandoned of his people for the multitude
of his enemies which oppressed them, when he might no
longer sustain the shot of darts and arrows, he boldly
lept into the sea, and diving under the water, escaped
the shot and swam the space of two hundred paces to one
of his ships, drawing his coat armor with his teeth after
him, that his enemies should not attain it, and also that
it might somewhat defend him from their arrows—and
that more marvel was, holding in his hand above the
water certain letters which a little before he had received
from the Senate!

Before him Sertorius, who of the Spaniards was named
the second Hannibal for his prowess, in the battle that
Scipio fought against the Cimbri, which invaded France,
Sertorius, when by negligence of his people his enemies

---

[11] powerful   [12] had not

prevailed and put his host to the worse, he, being sore wounded, and his horse being lost, armed as he was in a gesseron,[13] holding in his hands a target[14] and his sword, he lept into the river of Rhone, which is wonderful swift, and swimming against the stream, came to his company, not without great wondering of all his enemies, which stood and beheld him.

The great King Alexander lamented that he had not learned to swim, for in India, when he went against the puissant King Porus, he was constrained, in following his enterprise, to convey his host over a river of wonderful greatness; then caused he his horsemen to gauge the water, whereby he first perceived that it came to the breasts of the horses, and in the middle of the stream the horses went in water to the neck; wherewith the footmen being afeared, none of them durst adventure to pass over the river. That perceiving, Alexander with a dolorous manner in this wise lamented: "O how most unhappy am I of all other, that have not or[15] this time learned to swim!" And therewith he pulled a target from one of his soldiers, and casting it into the water, standing on it, with his spear conveyed himself with the stream, and governing the target wisely, brought himself unto the other side of the water. Whereof his people being abashed, some assayed to swim, some holding fast by the horses, other by spears and other like weapons, many upon fardels[16] and trusses,[17] got over the river; in so much as nothing was perished save a little baggage, and of that no great quantity lost.

What utility was showed to be in swimming at the first wars which the Romans had against the Carthagin-

---

[13] coat of mail   [14] shield
[15] before   [16] packs
[17] bundles

ians! It happened a battle to be on the sea between them, where they of Carthage, being vanquished, would have set up their sails to have fled, but that, perceiving divers young Romans, they threw themselves into the sea, and swimming unto the ships, they enforced their enemies to that the captain of the Romans, called Luctatius, might strike on land, and there assaulted them so asprely[18] easily take them.

Now behold what excellent commodity is in the feat of swimming, since no king, be he never so puissant or perfect in the experience of wars, may assure himself from the necessities which fortune soweth among men that be mortal. And since on the health and safeguard of a noble captain oftentimes dependeth the weal[19] of a realm, nothing should be kept from his knowledge whereby his person may be in every jeopardy preserved.

Among these exercises, it shall be convenient to learn to handle sundry weapons, specially the sword and the battle axe, which be for a nobleman most convenient. But the most honorable exercise, in mine opinion, and that beseemeth[20] the estate of every noble person, is to ride surely and clean on a great horse and a rough, which undoubtedly not only importeth a majesty and dread to inferior persons, beholding him above the common course of other men, daunting a fierce and cruel beast, but also is no little succor, as well in pursuit of enemies and confounding them as in escaping imminent danger when wisdom thereto exhorteth. Also a strong and hardy horse doth sometime more damage, under his master, than he with all his weapon; and also setteth forward the stroke, and causeth it to light with more violence.

Bucephalus, the horse of great King Alexander, who

[18] roughly   [19] well-being, safety
[20] becomes

suffered none on his back save only his master, at the battle of Thebes, being sore wounded, would not suffer the king to depart from him to another horse, but persisting in his furious courage, wonderfully continued out the battle, with his feet and teeth beating down and destroying many enemies. And many semblable[21] marvels of his strength he showed; wherefore Alexander, after the horse was slain, made in remembrance of him a city in the country of India and called it Bucephalia, in perpetual memory of so worthy a horse, which in his life had so well served him.

What wonderful enterprises did Julius Caesar achieve by the help of his horse, which not only did excel all other horses in fierceness and swift running, but also was in some part discrepant in figure from other horses, having his fore hooves like to the feet of a man! And in that figure Pliny writeth that he saw him carved before the temple of Venus. Other remembrance there is of divers horses by whose monstrous power men did exploit incredible affairs. But because the report of them containeth things impossible, and is not written by any approved author, I will not in this place rehearse them— saving that it is yet supposed that the castle of Arundel in Sussex was made by one Beauvize,[22] Earl of Southampton, for a monument of his horse called Arundel, which in far countries had saved his master from many perils.

Now considering the utility in riding great horses, it shall be necessary (as I have said) that a gentleman do learn to ride a great and fierce horse whiles he is tender and the brawn and sinews of his thighs not fully consolidate.

There is also a right good exercise which is also expedient to learn: which is named the vaunting of a horse,

[21] similar   [22] Bevis

that is, to leap on him at every side without stirrup or other help, specially whiles the horse is going; and being therein expert, then armed at all points to assay the same, the commodity whereof is so manifest that I need no further to declare it.

18

The Ancient Hunting of Greeks and Romans

But now will I proceed to write of exercises which be not utterly reproved of noble authors if they be used with opportunity and in measure—I mean hunting, hawking, and dancing. In hunting may be an imitation of battle, if it be such as was used among them of Persia; whereof Xenophon, the noble and most eloquent philosopher, maketh a delectable mention in his book called the *Doctrine of Cyrus,* and also maketh another special book containing the whole discipline of the ancient hunting of the Greeks; and in that form being used, it is a laudable exercise, of the which I will now somewhat write.

Cyrus and other ancient kings of Persia (as Xenophon writeth) used this manner in all their hunting. First, whereas it seemeth there was in the realm of Persia but one city, which as I suppose was called Persepolis, there were the children of the Persians from their infancy unto the age of seventeen years brought up in the learning of justice and temperance, and also to observe continence in meat and drink, in so much that, whithersoever they went, they took with them for their sustenance but only bread and herbs, called kersis, in Latin *nasturtium,* and for their drink, a dish to take water out of the rivers as they passed. Also they learned to shoot and to cast the dart or javelin. When they came to the age of seventeen years, they were lodged in the palaces that were there ordained for the king and his nobles, which was as well for the safeguard of the city as for the example of temperance that they daily had at their eyes given to them by the nobles (which also might be called peers, by the signification of the Greek word, wherein they were called *homotimoi*). Moreover they were accustomed to rise alway in the first spring of the day, and patiently to sustain alway both cold and heat. And the king did see them exercised in going and also in running. And when he intended in his own person to hunt, which he did commonly every month, he took with him the one half of the company of young men that were in the palaces. Then took every man with him his bow and quiver with arrows, his sword or hache[1] of steel, a little target,[2] and two darts. The bow and arrows served to pursue beasts that were swift, and the darts to assail them and all other beasts. And when their courage was chafed,[3] or that by fierceness of the beast they were in danger, then force constrained them to strike with the sword or hache, and to have good eye at the violent assault of the beast, and to defend them if need were with their targets. Wherein they accounted to be the truest and most certain meditation[4] of wars. And to this hunting the king did conduct them, and he himself first hunted such beasts as he happened to encounter. And when he had taken his pleasure, he then with most diligence did set other forward, beholding who hunted valiantly and reforming them whom he saw negligent or slothful. But ere they went forth to this hunting, they dined competently; and during their hunting they dined no more—for if for any occasion their hunting continued above one day, they took the said dinner for their supper; and the next day, if they killed no game, they hunted until suppertime, accounting those

---

[1] battle axe   [2] shield
[3] became hot   [4] study

two days but for one. And if they took anything, they ate it at their supper with joy and pleasure. If nothing were killed, they ate only bread and kersis, as I before rehearsed, and drank thereto water. And if any man will dispraise this diet, let him think what pleasure there is in bread to him that is hungry, and what delectation is in drinking water to him that is thirsty.

Surely this manner of hunting may be called a necessary solace and pastime, for therein is the very imitation of battle: for not only it doth show the courage and strength as well of the horse as of him that rideth—traversing over mountains and valleys, encountering and overthrowing great and mighty beasts—but also it increaseth in them both agility and quickness, also sleight and policy to find such passages and straits where they may prevent or entrap their enemies. Also by continuance therein, they shall easily sustain travail in wars, hunger and thirst, cold and heat. Hitherto be the words of Xenophon, although I have not set them in like order as he wrote them.

The chief hunting of the valiant Greeks was at the lion, the leopard, the tiger, the wild swine, and the bear, and sometime the wolf and the hart. Theseus, which was companion to Hercules, attained the greatest part of his renown for fighting with the great boar, which the Greeks called *Phera*,[5] that wasted and consumed the fields of a great country.

Meleager likewise, for slaying of the great boar in Caledonia, which in greatness and fierceness exceeded all other boars, and had slain many noble and valiant persons.

The great Alexander, in times vacant from battle, delighted in that manner hunting. On a time he fought

[5] That is, Phaea, the monstrous sow of Crommyon, in Attica

alone with a lion wonderful great and fierce, [there] being present among other strangers the ambassador of Lacedaemonia; and after long travail, with incredible might, he overthrew the lion and slew him; whereat the said ambassador, wondering marvelously, said to the king: "I would to God (noble prince) ye should fight with a lion for some great empire." By which words it seemed that he nothing approved the valiantness of a prince by fighting with a wild beast, wherein much more was adventured than might be by the victory gotten.

Albeit Pompey, Sertorius, and divers other noble Romans, when they were in Numidia, Libya, and such other countries, which now be called Barbary and Morisco,[6] in the vacation season from wars, they hunted lions, leopards, and such other beasts fierce and savage, to the intent thereby to exercise themselves and their soldiers. But Almighty God be thanked, in this realm be no such cruel beasts to be pursued! Notwithstanding, in the hunting of red deer and fallow[7] might be a great part of semblable[8] exercise used by noblemen, specially in forests which be spacious—if they would use but a few number of hounds, only to harborowe[9] or rouse the game, and by their yorning[10] to give knowledge which way it fleeth, the remnant of the disport to be in pursuing with javelins and other weapons, in manner of war. And to them which in this hunting do show most prowess and activity, a garland or some other like token to be given in sign of victory, and with a joyful manner to be brought in the presence of him that is chief in the company, there to receive condign[11] praise for their good endeavor. I

---

[6] Morocco	[7] a species of deer
[8] similar	[9] trace
[10] crying or baying (?)	[11] deserved

dispraise not the hunting of the fox with running hounds, but it is not to be compared to the other hunting in commodity of exercise. Therefore it would be used in the deep winter, when the other game is unseasonable.

Hunting of the hare with greyhounds is a right good solace for men that be studious; or them to whom nature hath not given personage[12] or courage apt for the wars. And also for gentlewomen which fear neither sun nor wind for appairing[13] their beauty. And peradventure they shall be thereat less idle than they should be at home in their chambers.

Killing of deer with bows or greyhounds serveth well for the pot (as is the common saying), and therefore it must of necessity be sometime used. But it containeth therein no commendable solace or exercise, in comparison to the other form of hunting, if it be diligently perceived.

As for hawking, I can find no notable remembrance that it was used of ancient time among noble princes. I call ancient time before a thousand years past, since which time virtue and nobleness hath rather decayed than increased. Nor I could never know who found first that disport.

Pliny maketh mention in his eighth book of the history of nature that in the parts of Greece called Thrace, men and hawks, as it were by a confederacy, took birds together in this wise: the men sprang the birds out of the bushes, and the hawks, soaring over them, beat them down, so that the men might easily take them. And then did the men depart[14] equally the prey with the falcons, which, being well served, eftsoons[15] and of a custom repaired to such places where, being aloft, they perceived

[12] bodily frame
[14] share
[13] impairing
[15] straightway

men to that purpose assembled. By which rehearsal of
Pliny, we may conject[16] that from Thrace came this disport of hawking. And I doubt not but many other, as
well as I, have seen a semblable experience of wild
hobies,[17] which in some countries that be champaine[18]
will soar and lie aloft, hovering over larks and quails,
and keep them down on the ground, whiles they which
await on the prey do take them.

But in what wise or wheresoever the beginning of
hawking was, surely it is a right delectable solace, though
thereof cometh not so much utility (concerning exercise)
as there doth of hunting. But I would our falcons might
be satisfied with the division of their prey as the falcons
of Thrace were, that they needed not to devour and consume the hens of this realm in such number that, unneth[19] it be shortly considered, and that falcons be
brought to a more homely diet, it is right likely that
within a short space of years our familiar[20] poultry shall
be as scarce as be now partridge and pheasant. I speak
not this in dispraise of the falcons, but of them which
keepeth them like coknayes.[21] The mean[22] gentlemen
and honest householders which care for the gentle entertainment of their friends do find in their dish that I say
truth, and noblemen shall right shortly espy it when they
come suddenly to their friend's house, unpurveyed[23] for
lack of long warning.

But now to return to my purpose. Undoubtedly hawking, measurably used and for a pastime, giveth to a man
good appetite to his supper. And at the least way with-

[16] conjecture
[17] small species of falcon
[18] level, open country
[19] unless (?)
[20] domestic
[21] pampered pets
[22] ordinary (?)
[23] without provision

draweth him from other dalliance or disports dishonest, and to body and soul perchance pernicious.

Now I purpose to declare something concerning dancing, wherein is merit of praise and dispraise, as I shall express it in such form as I trust the reader shall find therein a rare and singular pleasure, with also good learning in things not yet commonly known in our vulgar.[24] Which if it be read of him that hath good opportunity and quiet silence, I doubt not but he shall take thereby such commodity as he looked not to have found in that exercise, which of the more part of sad[25] men is so little esteemed.

[24] vulgar tongue (that is, English)   [25] grave

19

That All Dancing Is Not to Be Reproved

I am not of that opinion that all dancing generally is repugnant unto virtue, although some persons excellently learned, specially divines, so do affirm it, which alway have in their mouths (when they come into the pulpit) the saying of the noble doctor Saint Augustine, that "Better it were to delve[1] or to go to plow on the Sunday than to dance." Which might be spoken of that kind of dancing which was used in the time of Saint Augustine, when everything with the empire of Rome declined from their perfection; and the old manner of dancing was forgotten, and none remained but that which was lascivious, and corrupted the minds of them that danced, and provoked sin, as semblably[2] some do at this day. Also at that time idolatry was not clearly extinct, but divers fragments thereof remained in every region. And perchance solempne[3] dances, which were celebrate unto the paynyms'[4] false gods, were yet continued; for as much as the pure religion of Christ was not in all places consolidate, and the pastors and curates did wink at such recreations, fearing that if they should hastily have removed it, and induced suddenly the severity of God's laws, they should stir the people thereby to a general sedition, to the imminent danger and subversion of Christ's whole religion, late

[1] dig
[3] solemn
[2] similarly
[4] pagans'

sown among them, and not yet sufficiently rooted. But the wise and discreet doctor Saint Augustine, using the art of an orator, wherein he was right excellent, omitting all rigorous menace or terror, dissuaded them by the most easiest way from that manner ceremony belonging to idolatry, preferring before it bodily occupation,[5] thereby aggravating the offense to God that was in that ceremony—since occupation, which is necessary for man's sustenance, and in due times virtuous, is notwithstanding prohibited to be used on the Sundays.

And yet in these words of this noble doctor is not so general dispraise to all dancing as some men do suppose. And that for two causes. First, in his comparison he preferreth not before dancing, or joineth thereto, any vicious exercise, but annecteth[6] it with tilling and digging of the earth, which be labors incident to man's living, and in them is contained nothing that is vicious. Wherefore the pre-eminence thereof above dancing, qualifying the offense they being done[7] out of due time—that is to say in an holy day—concludeth not dancing to be at all times and in every manner unlawful or vicious: considering that in certain cases of extreme necessity, men might both plow and delve without doing to God any offense. Also it shall seem to them that seriously do examine the said words, that therein Saint Augustine doth not prohibit dancing so generally as it is taken, but only such dances which (as I late said) were superstitious, and contained in them a spice of idolatry, or else did with unclean motions or countenances irritate the minds of the dancers to venereal lusts. Whereby fornication and avoutry[8] were daily increased. Also in those dances were

[5] labor   [6] joins
[7] if they are done   [8] adultery

interlaced ditties of wanton love or ribaudry,[9] with frequent remembrance of the most vile idols, Venus and Bacchus, as it were that the dance were to their honor and memory which most of all abhorred[10] from Christ's religion, savoring the ancient error or paganism.

I would to God those names were not at this day used in ballads and ditties in the courts of princes and noblemen, where many good wits[11] be corrupted with semblable fantasies, which, in better wise employed, might have been more necessary to the public weal and their prince's honor. But now will I leave this serious matter to divines, to persuade or dissuade herein according to their offices. And since in mine opinion Saint Augustine, that blessed clerk,[12] reproveth not so generally all dancing but that I may lawfully rehearse some kind thereof which may be necessary and also commendable, taking it for an exercise, I shall now proceed to speak of the first beginning thereof, and in how great estimation it was had in divers regions.

[9] ribaldry

[11] minds

[10] shrank with horror

[12] churchman

20

Of the First Beginning of Dancing and the Old Estimation Thereof

There be sundry opinions of the original beginning of dancing. The poets do feign that when Saturn, which devoured divers his children, and semblably[1] would have done with Jupiter, Rhea the mother of Jupiter devised that *Curetes* (which were men of arms in that country) should dance in armor, playing with their swords and shields in such form as, by that new and pleasant device, they should assuage the melancholy of Saturn; and in the meantime, Jupiter was conveyed into Phrygia, where, Saturn also pursuing him, Rhea semblably taught the people there called *Coribantes* to dance in another form, wherewith Saturn was eftsoons[2] demulced[3] and appeased. Which fable hath a resemblance to the history of the Bible, in the first book of Kings, where it is remembered that Saul (whom God chose, from a keeper of asses, to be king of Jews, who in stature excelled and was above all other men by the head), declining from the laws and precepts of God, was possessed of an evil spirit, which oftentimes tormented and vexed him; and other remedy found he none but that David, which after him was king, being at that time a proper child, and playing sweetly on a harp, with his pleasant and perfect harmony reduced his

[1] likewise   [2] straightway
[3] soothed

mind into his pristinate[4] estate; and during the time that
he played, the spirit ceased to vex him. Which I suppose
happened not only of the efficacy of music (albeit therein
is much power, as well in repressing as exciting natural
affects[5]) but also of the virtue ingenerate in the child
David that played, whom God also had predestinate to
be a great king and a great prophet. And for the sovereign gifts of grace and of nature that he was endowed
with, Almighty God said of him that he had found a man
after his heart and pleasure. But now to return to speak
of dancing.

Some interpreters of poets do imagine that Proteus,
who is supposed to have turned himself into sundry figures—as sometime to show himself like a serpent, sometime like a lion, other whiles like water, another time
like the flame of fire—signifieth to be none other but a
deliver[6] and crafty dancer, which in his dance could
imagine the inflections of the serpent, the soft and delectable flowing of the water, the swiftness and mounting
of the fire, the fierce rage of the lion, the violence and
fury of the leopard. Which exposition is not to be dispraised, since it discordeth not from reason. But one
opinion there is which I will rehearse, more for the merry
fantasy that therein is contained than for any faith or
credit that is to be given thereto.

Over Syracuse (a great and ancient city in Sicily) there
reigned a cruel tyrant called Hiero, which by horrible
tyrannies and oppressions brought himself into the indignation and hatred of all his people; which he perceiving, lest by mutual communication they should conspire
against him any rebellion, he prohibited all men under
terrible menaces that no man or woman should speak

[4] former   [5] emotions
[6] nimble

unto another, but instead of words, they should use—in their necessary affairs—countenances, tokens,[7] and movings with their feet, hands, and eyes; which for necessity first used, at the last grew to a perfect and delectable dancing. And Hiero, notwithstanding his foolish curiosity,[8] at the last was slain of his people most miserably. But although this history were true, yet was not dancing at this time first begun, for Orpheus and Musaeus, the most ancient of poets, and also Homer, which were long afore Hiero, do make mention of dancing. And in Delos, which was the most ancient temple of Apollo, no solemnity was done without dancing.

Also in India, where the people honoreth the sun, they assemble together, and when the sun first appeareth, joined all in a dance, they salute him, supposing that for as much as he moveth without sensible noise, it pleaseth him best to be likewise saluted—that is to say, with a pleasant motion and silence. The interpreters of Plato do think that the wonderful and incomprehensible order of the celestial bodies (I mean stars and planets) and their motions harmonical gave to them that[9] intentifly,[10] and by the deep search of reason, behold their courses—in the sundry diversities of number and time—a form of imitation of a semblable[11] motion which they called dancing or saltation. Wherefore the more near they approached to that temperance and subtle modulation of the said superior bodies, the more perfect and commendable is their dancing; which is most like to the truth of any opinion that I have hitherto founden.

Other fables there be which I omit for this present time. And now I will express in what estimation dancing

[7] signs
[8] carefulness
[9] who
[10] attentively
[11] similar

was had in the ancient time, and also sundry forms of dancing—not all, but such as had in them a semblance of virtue or cunning.

When the ark of God (wherein was put the tables of the commandments, the yard[12] wherewith Moses divided the Red Sea and did the miracles in the presence of Pharaoh, King of Egypt, also a part of manna wherewith the children of Israel were fed forty years in desert) was recovered of the Philistines and brought unto the city of Gaba, the holy King David, wearing on him a linen surplice, danced before the said ark, following him a great number of instruments of music; whereat his wife Michal, the daughter of King Saul, disdained and scorned him; wherewith (as Holy Scripture saith) Almighty God was much displeased. And David, not ceasing, danced joyously through the city, in that manner honoring that solemn feast which among the Jews was one of the chief and principal; wherewith God was more pleased than with all the other observances that then were done unto him at that time.

I will not trouble the readers with the innumerable ceremonies of the Gentiles which were comprehended in dancings, since they ought to be numbered among superstitions. But I will declare how wise men and valiant captains embraced dancing for a sovereign and profitable exercise.

Lycurgus, that gave first laws to the Lacedaemonians (a people in Greece), ordained that the children there should be taught as diligently to dance in armor as to fight; and that in time of wars, they should move them in battle against their enemies in form and manner of dancing.

Semblably the old inhabitants of Ethiopia, at the join-

[12] rod

ing of their battles, and when the trumpets and other instruments sound, they dance; and instead of a quiver,
they have their darts set about their bodies, like to rays
or beams of the sun; wherewith they believe that they
put their enemies in fear. Also it was not lawful for any
of them to cast any dart at his enemy but[13] dancing. And
not only this rude people esteemed so much dancing,
but also the most noble of the Greeks, which for their
excellency in prowess and wisdom were called half-gods,
as Achilles, and his son Pyrrhus, and divers other. Wherefore Homer, among the high benefits that God giveth to
man, he reciteth dancing. For he saith in the first book
of *Iliados:*

> God granteth to some man prowess martial,
> To another dancing, with song harmonical.

Suppose ye that the Romans, which in gravity of manners passed the Greeks, had not great pleasure in dancing? Did not Romulus, the first king of Romans, and
builder of the city of Rome, ordain certain priests and
ministers to the god Mars (whom he advaunted[14] to be
his father)? Which priests, for as much as certain times
they danced about the city with targets,[15] that they
imagined to fall from heaven, were called in Latin *Salii*
(which into English may be translated dancers), who continued so long time in reverence among the Romans that
unto the time that they were christened, the noblemen
and princes' children there, using much diligence and
suit, coveted to be of the college of the said dancers.

Moreover the emperors that were most noble delighted
in dancing, perceiving therein to be a perfect measure,
which may be called modulation; wherein some dancers

[13] except while   [14] boasted
[15] shields

of old time so wonderfully excelled that they would
plainly express in dancing, without any words or ditty,
histories with the whole circumstance of affairs in them
contained; whereof I shall rehearse two marvelous ex-
periences.

At Rome in the time of Nero there was a philosopher
called Demetrius, which was of that sect that, for as much
as they abandoned all shamefastness in their words and
acts, they were called *Cynici* (in English, doggish). This
Demetrius, often reproving dancing, would say that there
was nothing therein of any importance, and that it was
none other but a counterfeiting with the feet and hands
of the harmony that was showed before in the rebeck,[16]
shawn,[17] or other instrument; and that the motions were
but vain and separate from all understanding, and of no
purpose or efficacy. Whereof hearing, a famous dancer,
and one (as it seemed) that was not without good learning and had in remembrance many histories, he came to
Demetrius and said unto him: "Sir, I humbly desire you
refuse not to do me that honesty[18] with your presence in
beholding me dance, which ye shall see me do without
sound of any instrument. And then if it shall seem to you
worthy dispraise, utterly banish and confound[19] my science."[20] Whereunto Demetrius granted. The young
man danced the advoutry[21] of Mars and Venus, and
therein expressed how Vulcan, husband to Venus, thereof
being advertised[22] by the sun, laid snares for his wife and
Mars; also how they were wound and tied in Vulcan's
net; moreover how all the gods came to the spectacle;
finally how Venus, all ashamed and blushing, fearfully

---

[16] a kind of fiddle   [17] an oboe-like instrument
[18] respect   [19] destroy
[20] art   [21] adultery
[22] notified

desired her lover Mars to deliver her from that peril; and the residue contained in the fable. Which he did with so subtle and crafty gesture, with such perspicuity and declaration of every act in the matter (which of all thing is most difficile[23]), with such a grace and beauty, also with a wit so wonderful and pleasant that Demetrius (as it seemed), thereat rejoicing and delighting, cried with a loud voice: "O man, I do not only see, but also hear what thou doest! And it seemeth also to me that with thy hands thou speakest!" Which saying was confirmed by all them that were at that time present.

The same young man sang and danced on a time before the emperor Nero, when there was also present a strange king, which understood none other language but of his own country; yet notwithstanding, the man danced so aptly and plainly, as his custom was, that the strange king, although he perceived not what he said, yet he understood every deal of the matter. And when he had taken his leave of the emperor to depart, the emperor offered to give to him anything that he thought might be to his commodity. "Ye may," said the king, "bounteously reward me if ye lend me the young man that danced before your majesty." Nero, wondering and requiring of him why he so importunately desired the dancer, or what commodity the dancer might be unto him, "Sir," said the king, "I have divers confines[24] and neighbors that be of sundry languages and manners; wherefore I have oftentimes need of many interpreters. Wherefore if I had this man with me, and should have anything to do with my neighbors, he would so with his fashion and gesture express everything to me, and teach them to do the same, that from henceforth I should not have need of any interpreter."

[23] difficult   [24] regions

Also the ancient philosophers commended dancing: in so much as Socrates, the wisest of all the Greeks in his time, and from whom all the sects of philosophers, as from a fountain, were derived, was not ashamed to account dancing among the serious disciplines, for the commendable beauty, for the apt and proportionate moving, and for the crafty disposition and fashioning of the body. It is to be considered that in the said ancient time there were divers manners of dancing, which varied in the names likewise as they did in tunes of the instrument, as semblably we have at this day. But those names, some were general, some were special. The general names were given of the universal form of dancing, whereby was represented the qualities or conditions of sundry estates: as the majesty of princes was showed in that dance which was named *eumelia,* and belonged to tragedies; dissolute motions and wanton countenances, in that which was called *cordax,* and pertained to comedies, wherein men of base havior[25] only danced. Also the form of battle and fighting in armor was expressed in those dances which were called *enopliae.* Also there was a kind of dancing called *hormus,* of all the other most like to that which is at this time used—wherein danced young men and maidens, the man expressing, in his motion and countenance, fortitude and magnanimity apt for the wars; the maiden, moderation and shamefastness: which represented a pleasant connection of fortitude and temperance. Instead of these we have now base dances, bargenettes, pavions, turgions, and rounds. And as for the special names, they were taken as they be now, either of the names of the first inventors, or of the measure and number that they do contain, or of the first words of the ditty which the song comprehendeth whereof the dance was

[25] deportment

made. In every of the said dances there was a concinnity[26] of moving the foot and body, expressing some pleasant or profitable affects or motions of the mind.

Here a man may behold what artifice and craft there was in the ancient time in dancing, which at this day no man can imagine or conject.[27] But if men would now apply the first part of their youth—that is to say, from seven years to twenty—effectually in the sciences liberal and knowledge of histories, they should revive the ancient form as well of dancing as of other exercises. Whereof they might take not only pleasure, but also profit and commodity.

[26] harmony   [27] conjecture

21

Wherefore in the Good Order of Dancing a Man and a Woman Danceth Together

It is diligently to be noted that the associating of man and woman in dancing, they both observing one number and time in their movings, was not begun without a special consideration, as well for the necessary conjunction of those two persons as for the intimation of sundry virtues which be by them represented. And for as much as by the association of a man and a woman in dancing may be signified matrimony, I could in declaring the dignity and commodity of that sacrament make entire volumes—if it were not so commonly known to all men that almost every frere lymitour[1] carrieth it written in his bosom. Wherefore lest in repeating a thing so frequent and common, my book should be as fastidious[2] or fulsome to the readers as such merchant preachers be now to their customers, I will reverently take my leave of divines. And for my part, I will endeavor myself to assemble out of the books of ancient poets and philosophers matter as well apt to my purpose as also new, or at the least ways infrequent or seldom heard of them that have not read very many authors in Greek and Latin.

But now to my purpose. In every dance of a most ancient custom there danceth together a man and a woman, holding each other by the hand or the arm: which betokeneth concord. Now it behooveth the danc-

---

[1] friar licensed to beg within a definite limit
[2] distasteful, boring

ers, and also the beholders of them, to know all qualities incident to a man, and also all qualities to a woman like-wise appertaining.

A man in his natural perfection is fierce, hardy, strong in opinion, covetous of glory, desirous of knowledge, appetiting[3] by generation[4] to bring forth his semblable.[5] The good nature of a woman is to be mild, timorous, tractable, benign, of sure remembrance, and shamefast. Divers other qualities of each of them might be found out, but these be most apparent, and for this time suffi-cient.

Wherefore when we behold a man and a woman danc-ing together, let us suppose there to be a concord of all the said qualities, being joined together as I have set them in order. And the moving of the man would be more vehement, of the woman more delicate, and with less advancing of the body: signifying the courage and strength that ought to be in a man, and the pleasant soberness that should be in a woman. And in this wise *fierceness* joined with *mildness* maketh *severity; audacity* with *timorosity* maketh *magnanimity;* willful opinion and *tractability* (which is to be shortly persuaded and moved) maketh *constance,* a virtue; *covetousness of glory* adorned with *benignity* causeth honor; *desire of knowl-edge,* with *sure remembrance,* procureth *sapience; shame-fastness* joined to *appetite of generation* maketh *conti-nence,* which is a mean between *chastity* and *inordinate lust.* These qualities, in this wise being knit together, and signified in the personages of man and woman danc-ing, do express or set out the figure of very[6] nobility, which, in the higher estate it is contained, the more ex-cellent is the virtue in estimation.

[3] craving instinctively   [4] procreation
[5] likeness   [6] true

22

How Dancing May Be an Introduction unto the First Moral Virtue, Called Prudence

As I have already affirmed, the principal cause of this my little enterprise is to declare an induction or mean[s] how children of gentle nature or disposition may be trained into the way of virtue with a pleasant facility; and for as much as it is very expedient that there be mixed with study some honest and moderate disport, or at the least way recreation, to recomfort and quicken the vital spirits, lest they long travailing, or being much occupied in contemplation or remembrance of things grave and serious, might happen to be fatigate[1] or perchance oppressed. And therefore Tully,[2] who unneth[3] found ever any time vacant from study, permitteth in his first book *Of Offices* that men may use play and disport; yet notwithstanding, in such wise as they do use sleep and other manner of quiet, when they have sufficiently disposed earnest matters and of weighty importance.

Now because there is no pastime to be compared to that wherein may be found both recreation and meditation of virtue, I have, among all honest pastimes wherein is exercise of the body, noted dancing to be of an excellent utility, comprehending in it wonderful figures (or, as the Greeks do call them, *ideae*) of virtues and noble quali-

[1] fatigued   [2] Cicero
[3] hardly

tics; and specially of the commodious virtue called prudence, whom Tully defineth to be the knowledge of
things which ought to be desired and followed, and also
of them which ought to be fled from or eschewed. And it
is named of Aristotle the mother of virtues; of other
philosophers it is called the captain or mistress of virtues;
of some, the housewife, for as much as by her diligence
she doth investigate and prepare places apt and convenient where other virtues shall execute their powers or
offices. Wherefore as Solomon saith, like as in water be
showed the visages of them that behold it, so unto men
that be prudent, the secrets of men's hearts be openly discovered. This virtue being so commodious to man, and
as it were the porch of the noble palace of man's reason
whereby all other virtues shall enter, it seemeth to me right
expedient that as soon as opportunity may be founden,
a child or young man be thereto induced. And because
that the study of virtue is tedious for the more part to
them that do flourish in young years, I have devised how
in the form of dancing now late used in this realm among
gentlemen the whole description of this virtue prudence
may be found out and well perceived, as well by the dancers as by them which, standing by, will be diligent beholders and markers, having first mine instruction surely
graven in the table[4] of their remembrance. Wherefore all
they that have their courage[5] stirred toward very[6] honor
or perfect nobility, let them approach to this pastime,
and either themselves prepare them to dance, or else at
the least way behold with watching eyes other that can
dance truly, keeping just measure and time. But to the
understanding of this instruction they must mark well

[4] tablet   [5] spirit
[6] true

the sundry motions and measures which in true form of dancing is to be specially observed.

The first moving in every dance is called honor, which is a reverent inclination or curtsy, with a long deliberation or pause, and is but one motion comprehending the time of three other motions or setting forth of the foot. By that may be signified that at the beginning of all our acts we should do due honor to God, which is the root of prudence; which honor is compact of these three things: fear, love, and reverence. And that in the beginning of all things we should advisedly, with some tract of time, behold and foresee the success of our enterprise.

By the second motion, which is two in number, may be signified celerity[7] and slowness; which two, albeit they seem to discord in their effects and natural properties— and therefore they may be well resembled to the brawl in dancing (for in our English tongue we say men do brawl when between them is altercation in words)—yet of them two springeth an excellent virtue, whereunto we lack a name in English. Wherefore I am constrained to usurp a Latin word, calling it *maturity;* which word, though it be strange and dark, yet by declaring the virtue in a few more words, the name once brought in custom shall be as facile[8] to understand as other words late comen out of Italy and France and made denizens among us.

Maturity is a mean between two extremities, wherein nothing lacketh or exceedeth; and is in such estate that it may neither increase nor minish[9] without losing the denomination of maturity. The Greeks in a proverb do express it properly in two words, which I can none otherwise interpret in English but "speed thee slowly."

Also of this word "maturity" sprang a noble and pre-

7 swiftness   8 easy
9 diminish

cious sentence, recited by Sallust in the battle against Cati-
line, which is in this manner or like: "Consult before thou
enterprise anything; and after thou hast taken counsel, it
is expedient to do it maturely." *Maturum* in Latin may
be interpreted ripe or ready: as fruit, when it is ripe, it is
at the very point to be gathered and eaten; and every
other thing, when it is ready, it is at the instant after to
be occupied. Therefore that word "maturity" is translated
to the acts of man, that when they be done with such
moderation that nothing in the doing may be seen superfluous or indigent,[10] we may say that they be maturely
done—reserving the words "ripe" and "ready" to fruit
and other things separate from affairs, as we have now in
usage. And this do I now remember for the necessary
augmentation of our language.

In the excellent and most noble emperor Octavius
Augustus, in whom reigned all nobility, nothing is more
commended than that he had frequently in his mouth
this word *matura,* do maturely—as he should have said,
do neither too much ne[11] too little, too soon ne too late,
too swiftly nor slowly, but in due time and measure.

Now I trust I have sufficiently expound the virtue
called maturity, which is the mean or mediocrity between
sloth and celerity, commonly called speediness; and so
have I declared what utility may be taken of a brawl in
dancing.

[10] deficient   [11] nor

23

The Third and Fourth Branches of Prudence

The third motion, called singles, is of two unities separate in passing forward—by whom may be signified providence and industry—which, after everything maturely achieved, as is before written, maketh the first pass forward in dancing. But it shall be expedient to expound what is the thing called providence, for as much as it is not known to every man.

Providence is whereby a man not only foreseeth commodity and incommodity, prosperity and adversity, but also consulteth, and therewith endeavoreth as well to repel annoyance as to attain and get profit and advantage. And the difference between it and consideration is that consideration only consisteth in pondering and examining things conceived in the mind, providence in helping them with counsel and act. Wherefore to consideration pertaineth excogitation and advisement; to providence, provision and execution. For like as the good husband,[1] when he hath sown his ground, setteth up clouts[2] or threads (which some call shailes, some blenchars, or other like shows) to fear away birds, which he foreseeth ready to devour and hurt his corn—also perceiving the improfitable weeds appearing, which will annoy his corn or herbs, forthwith he weedeth them clean out of his ground, and will not suffer them to grow or increase—semblably[3] it is

[1] farmer   [2] pieces of cloth
[3] likewise

the part of a wise man to foresee and provide that either in such things as he hath acquired by his study or diligence, or in such affairs as he hath in hand, he be not endamaged or impeached[4] by his adversaries. In like manner a governor of a public weal ought to provide as well by menaces as by sharp and terrible punishments that persons evil and improfitable do not corrupt and devour his good subjects. Finally there is in providence such an admiration and majesty that not only it is attributed to kings and rulers, but also to God, creator of the world.

"Industry" hath not been so long time used in the English tongue as "providence"; wherefore it is the more strange, and requireth the more plain exposition. It is a quality proceeding of wit[5] and experience, by the which a man perceiveth quickly, inventeth freshly, and counseleth speedily; wherefore they that be called industrious do most craftily and deeply understand in all affairs what is expedient, and by what means and ways they may soonest exploit them. And those things in whom other men travail,[6] a person industrious lightly and with facility[7] speedeth, and findeth new ways and means to bring to effect that he desireth. Among divers other remembered in histories, such one among the Greeks was Alcibiades, who, being in childhood most amiable of all other, and of most subtle wit, was instructed by Socrates. The said Alcibiades, by the sharpness of his wit, the doctrine[8] of Socrates, and by his own experience in sundry affairs in the common weal of the Athenians, became so industrious that, were it good or evil that he enterprised, nothing almost escaped that he achieved not, were the thing never

---

[4] obstructed   [5] intelligence
[6] labor   [7] ease
[8] teaching

so difficile[9] or (as who saith) impenetrable; and that many sundry things as well for his country as also against it, after that he for his inordinate pride and lechery was out of Athens exiled.

Among the Romans, Caius Julius Caesar, which first took upon him the perpetual rule and governance of the empire, is a noble example of industry, for in his incomparable wars and business incredible (if the authority and faith of the writers were not of long time approved), he did not only excogitate[10] most excellent policies and devices to vanquish or subdue his enemies, but also prosecuted them with such celerity[11] and effect that divers and many times he was in the camp of his enemies, or at the gates of their towns or fortresses, when they supposed that he and his host had been two days' journey from thence, leaving to them no time or leisure to consult or prepare against him sufficient resistance. And over that, this quality, industry, so reigned in him that he himself would minister to his secretaries, at one time and instant, the contents of three sundry epistles or letters. Also it is a thing wonderful to remember that he—being a prince of the most ancient and noble house of the Romans, and from the time that he came to man's estate almost continually in wars, also of glory insatiable, of courage invincible—could in affairs of such importance and difficulty, or (which is much more to be marveled at now) would so exactly write the history of his own acts and gests[12] that, for the native and inimitable eloquence in expressing the counsels, devices, conventions,[13] progressions, enterprises, exploitures,[14] forms, and fashions of

[9] difficult
[10] contrive
[11] speed
[12] exploits
[13] assemblies
[14] exploits

embattling, he seemeth to put all other writers of like matter to silence.

Here is the perfect pattern of industry, which I trust shall suffice to make the proper signification thereof to be understand of the readers, and consequently to incend[15] them to approach to the true practicing thereof.

So is the singles declared in these two qualities, providence and industry; which, seriously noted and often remembered of the dancers and beholders, shall acquire to[16] them no little fruit and commodity, if there be in their minds any good and laudable matter for virtue to work in.

[15] inflame   [16] gain

24

Of the Fifth Branch Called Circumspection, Showed in Reprinse

Commonly next after singles in dancing is a reprinse, which is one moving only, putting back the right foot to his fellow. And that may be well called circumspection, which signifieth as much as beholding on every part what is well and sufficient, what lacketh, how and from whence it may be provided; also what hath caused profit or damage in the time past, what is the estate of the time present, what advantage or peril may succeed or is imminent. And because in it is contained a deliberation, in having regard to that that followeth, and is also of affinity with providence and industry, I make him in the form of a retreat. In this motion a man may, as it were on a mountain or place of espial, behold on every side far off, measuring and esteeming everything; and either pursue it if it be commendable, or abandon it or eschew it if it be noyful.[1] This quality (like as providence and industry be) is a branch of prudence, which some call the princess of virtues; and it is not only expedient but also needful to every estate and degree of men that do continue in the life called active. In the *Iliados* of Homer, the noble duke Nestor, a man of marvelous eloquence and long experience, as he that lived three men's lives, as he there avaunteth[2] in the counsel that he gave to Agamemnon,

---

[1] annoying, noxious   [2] boasts

to reconcile to him Achilles, the most strong of all the Greeks, he persuaded Agamemnon specially to be circumspect: declaring how that the private contention between them should replenish[3] the host of the Greeks with much dolor; whereat King Priam and his children should laugh, and the residue of the Trojans in their minds should rejoice and take courage.

Among the Romans Quintus Fabius for this quality is sovereignly extolled among historians; and for that cause he is oftentimes called of them *Fabius Cunctator* (that is to say, the tarrier or delayer), for in the wars between the Romans and Hannibal, he, knowing all coasts of the country, continually kept him and his host on mountains and high places, within a small distance of Hannibal's army; so that neither he would abandon his enemies nor yet join with them battle. By which wonderful policy he caused Hannibal so to travail[4] that some time for lack of victual, and for weariness, great multitudes of his host perished. Also he oftentimes awaited them in dangerous places, unready, and then he skirmished with them, as long as he was sure to have of them advantage; and after, he repaired to the high places adjoining, using his accustomed manner to behold the passage of Hannibal. And by this means, this most circumspect captain Fabius wonderfully enfeebled the power of the said Hannibal; which is no less esteemed in praise than the subduing of Carthage by the valiant Scipio. For if Fabius had not so fatigate[5] Hannibal and his host, he had shortly subverted the city of Rome, and then could not Scipio have been able to attain that enterprise.

What more clear mirror or spectacle can we desire of circumspection than King Henry the Seventh, of most

[3] fill
[4] exert himself
[5] fatigued

noble memory, father unto our most dread sovereign lord, whose worthy renown, like the sun in the midst of his sphere, shineth and ever shall shine in men's remembrance? What incomparable circumspection was in him alway found, that—notwithstanding his long absence out of this realm; the disturbance of the same by sundry seditions among the nobility, civil wars and battles, wherein infinite people were slain, besides skirmishes and slaughters in the private contentions and factions of divers gentlemen; the laws laid in water (as is the proverb), affection[6] and avarice subduing justice and equity— yet by his most excellent wit[7] he in few years not only brought this realm in good order and under due obedience, revived the laws, advanced justice, refurnished his dominions, and repaired his manors; but also with such circumspection treated with other princes and realms, of leagues, of alliance, and amities that, during the more part of his reign, he was little or nothing inquieted[8] with outward hostility or martial business. And yet all other princes either feared him or had him in a fatherly reverence. Which praise, with the honor thereunto due, as inheritance descendeth by right unto his most noble son, our most dear sovereign lord that now presently reigneth. For as Tully[9] saith: "The best inheritance that the fathers leave to their children, excelling all other patrimony, is the glory or praise of virtue and noble acts." And of such fair inheritance his highness may compare with any prince that ever reigned; which he daily augmenteth, adding thereto other sundry virtues; which I forbear now to rehearse, to the intent I will exclude all suspicion of flattery, since I myself in this work do spe-

[6] passion
[8] disquieted, disturbed

[7] intelligence
[9] Cicero

cially reprove it. But that which is presently known, and is in experience, needeth no monument. And unto so excellent a prince there shall not lack hereafter condign[10] writers to register his acts with most eloquent style in perpetual remembrance.

[10] worthy

25

Of the Sixth, Seventh, and Eighth Branches of Prudence

A double in dancing is compact of the number of three, whereby may be noted these three branches of prudence: election, experience, and modesty. By them the said virtue of prudence is made complete and is in her perfection. Election is of an excellent power and authority, and hath such a majesty that she will not be approached unto of every man. For some there be to whom she denieth her presence, as children, natural fools, men being frantic or subdued with affects,[1] also they that be subjects to flatterers and proud men. In these persons reason lacketh liberty, which should prepare their entry unto election. This election, which is a part and as it were a member of prudence, is best described by opportunity, which is the principal part of counsel, and is compact of these things following: the importance of the thing consulted, the faculty and power of him that consulteth, the time when, the form how, the substance wherewith to do it, the dispositions and usages of the countries, for whom and against whom it ought to be done.

All these things prepensed[2] and gathered together seriously, and after a due examination every of them justly pondered in the balance of reason, immediately

---

[1] passions   [2] premeditated

cometh the authority of election, who taketh on her to appoint what is to be effectually followed or pursued, rejecting the residue. And then ought experience to be at hand, to whom is committed the actual execution. For without her, election is frustrate, and all invention of man is but a fantasy. And therefore who advisedly beholdeth the estate of man's life shall well perceive that all that ever was spoken or written was to be by experience executed; and to that intent was speech specially given to man, wherein he is most discrepant from brute beasts, in declaring what is good, what vicious, what is profitable, what improfitable by them which by clearness of wit do excel in knowledge to these that be of a more inferior capacity. And what utility should be acquired by such declaration if it should not be experienced with diligence?

The philosopher Socrates had not been named of Apollo the wisest man of all Greece if he had not daily practiced the virtues which he in his lessons commended.

Julius Caesar, the first emperor, although there were in him much hid learning—in so much as he first found the order of our calendar, with the cycle and bissext, called the leap year—yet is he not so much honored for his learning as he is for his diligence, wherewith he exploited or brought to conclusion those counsels which as well by his excellent learning and wisdom as by the advice of other expert counselors were before treated and (as I might say) ventilate.

Who will not repute it a thing vain and scornful, and more like to a May game than a matter serious or commendable, to behold a personage which in speech or writing expresseth nothing but virtuous manners, sage and discreet counsels, and holy advertisements[3] to be re-

[3] admonitions

solved into all vices, following in his acts nothing that he himself in his words approveth and teacheth to other?

Who shall anything esteem their wisdom which with great studies find out remedies and provisions necessary for things disordered or abused, and where they themselves may execute it, they leave it untouched; whereby their devices, with the sound that pronounced them, be vanished and come to nothing? Semblably[4] it is to be thought in all other doctrine.[5] Wherefore, as it seemed, it was not without consideration affirmed by Tully[6] that the knowledge and contemplation of nature's operations were lame and in a manner imperfect if there followed none actual experience. Of this shall be more spoken in the later end of this work.

Herewith would be conjoined, or rather mixed with it, the virtue called modesty: which by Tully is defined to be the knowledge of opportunity of things to be done or spoken, in appointing and setting them in time or place to them convenient and proper. Wherefore it seemeth to be much like to that which men commonly call discretion—albeit *discretio* in Latin signifieth separation, wherein it is more like to election; but as it is commonly used, it is not only like to modesty, but it is the self modesty. For he that forbeareth to speak, although he can do it both wisely and eloquently, because neither in the time nor in the hearers he findeth opportunity, so that no fruit may succeed of his speech, he therefore is vulgarly called a discreet person. Semblably they name him discreet that punisheth an offender less than his merits do require, having regard to the weakness of his person or to the aptness of his amendment. So do they in the virtue called liberality, where in giving is had considera-

⁴ Similarly   ⁵ learning
⁶ Cicero

tion as well of the condition and necessity of the person that receiveth as of the benefit that cometh of the gift received.

In every of these things and their semblable is modesty; which word, not being known in the English tongue, ne[7] of all them which understood Latin except they had read good authors, they improperly named this virtue discretion. And now some men do as much abuse the word "modesty" as the other did "discretion." For if a man have a sad countenance at all times, and yet not being moved with wrath, but patient, and of much gentleness, they which would be seen to be learned will say that the man is of a great modesty. Where they should rather say that he were of a great mansuetude:[8] which term, being semblably before this time unknown in our tongue, may be by the sufferance of wise men now received by custom, whereby the term shall be made familiar. That like as the Romans translated the wisdom of Greece into their city, we may, if we list,[9] bring the learnings and wisdoms of them both into this realm of England by the translation of their works, since like enterprise hath been taken by Frenchmen, Italians, and Germans, to our no little reproach for our negligence and sloth.

And thus I conclude the last part of dancing, which, diligently beholden, shall appear to be as well a necessary study as a noble and virtuous pastime, used and continued in such form as I hitherto have declared.

[7] nor
[8] gentleness, meekness
[9] desire

26

Of Other Exercises Which, If They Be
Moderately Used, Be to Every Estate
of Man Expedient

I have showed how hunting and dancing may be in the number of commendable exercises and pastimes not repugnant to virtue. And undoubted, it were much better to be occupied in honest recreation than to do nothing. For it is said of a noble author: "In doing nothing, men learn to do evil." And Ovid the poet saith:

> If thou flee idleness, Cupid hath no might:
> His bow lieth broken, his fire hath no light.

It is not only called idleness wherein the body or mind ceaseth from labor, but specially idleness is an omission of all honest exercise; the other may be better called a vacation from serious business, which was sometime embraced of wise men and virtuous. It is written to the praise of Xerxes King of Persia that in time vacant from the affairs of his realm, he with his own hands had planted innumerable trees, which long or[1] he died brought forth abundance of fruit; and for the crafty and delectable order in the setting of them, it was to all men, beholding the prince's industry, exceeding marvelous.

But who abhorreth not the history of Sardanapalus, king of the same realm, which, having in detestation all

[1] before

princely affairs, and leaving all company of men, enclosed
himself in chambers with a great multitude of concubines? And for that he would seem to be sometime occupied, or else that wanton pleasures and quietness became
to him tedious, he was found by one of his lords in a
woman's attire spinning in a distaff among persons de-
famed; which, known abroad, was to the people so odious
that finally by them he was burned, with all the place
whereto he fled for his refuge. And I suppose there is
not a more plain figure of idleness than playing at dice.
For besides that, that therein is no manner of exercise of
the body or mind, they which do play thereat must seem
to have no portion of wit[2] or cunning, if they will be
called fair players, or in some company avoid the stab of
a dagger, if they be taken with any crafty conveyance.[3]
And because alway wisdom is therein suspected, there is
seldom any playing at dice but thereat is vehement chiding and brawling, horrible oaths, cruel and sometime
mortal menaces. I omit strokes, which now and then do
happen oftentimes between brethren and most dear
friends, if fortune bring alway to one man evil chances,
which maketh the play of the other suspected. O why
should that be called a play which is compact of malice
and robbery?

Undoubtedly they that write of the first inventions of
things have good cause to suppose Lucifer, prince of
devils, to be the first inventor of dice playing, and Hell
the place where it was founded, although some do write
that it was first invented by Attalus. For what better
allective[4] could Lucifer devise to allure or bring men
pleasantly into damnable servitude than to purpose to
them, in form of a play, his principal treasury, wherein

[2] intelligence   [3] stealing
[4] enticement

the more part of sin is contained, and all goodness and virtue confounded?

The first occasion to play is tediousness of virtuous occupation. Immediately succeedeth coveting of another man's goods, which they call playing; thereto is annected[5] avarice and strait[6] keeping, which they call winning; soon after cometh swearing, in rending the members of God, which they name nobleness (for they will say he that sweareth deep, sweareth like a lord); then followeth fury or rage, which they call courage; among them cometh inordinate watch, which they name painfulness; he bringeth in gluttony, and that is good fellowship; and after cometh sleep superfluous, called among them natural rest; and he sometime bringeth in lechery, which is now named dalliance. The name of this treasury is verily idleness, the door whereof is left wide open to dice players; but if they hap to bring in their company learning, virtuous business, liberality, patience, charity, temperance, good diet, or shamefastness, they must leave them without the gates. For evil custom, which is the porter, will not suffer them to enter.

Alas what pity is it that any Christian man should by wanton company be trained[7]—I will no more say into this treasury, but into this loathsome dungeon, where he shall lie fettered in gyves[8] of ignorance, and bound with the strong chain of obstinacy, hard to be loosed but by grace!

The most noble emperor Octavius Augustus, who hath among writers in divers of his acts an honorable remembrance, only for playing at dice, and that but seldom, sustaineth in histories a note of reproach. The Lace-

---

[5] joined   [6] close
[7] drawn   [8] shackles

daemonians sent an ambassade to the city of Corinth, to
have with them alliance; but when the ambassadors
found the princes and counselors playing at dice, they departed without exploiting[9] their message, saying that they
would not maculate[10] the honor of their people with such
a reproach, to be said that they had made alliance with
dicers. Also to Demetrius, the king of Parthians sent
golden dice in the rebuke of his lightness.

Everything is to be esteemed after his value. But who,
hearing a man, whom he knoweth not, to be called a
dicer, anyone supposeth him not to be of light credence,
dissolute, vain, and remiss? Who almost trusteth his
brother, whom he knoweth a dice player? Yea, among
themselves they laugh when they perceive or hear any doctrine[11] or virtuous word proceed from any of their companions, thinking that it becometh not his person—much
more when he doth anything with devotion or wisdom.
How many gentlemen, how many merchants have in this
damnable pastime consumed their substance, as well by
their own labors as by their parents', with great study
and painful travail, in a long time acquired, and finished
their lives in debt and penury! How many goodly and
bold yeomen hath it brought unto theft, whereby they
have prevented[12] the course of nature, and died by the
order of laws miserably! These be the fruits and revenues
of that devilish merchandise, beside the final reward,
which is more terrible—the report whereof I leave to
divines,[13] such as fear not to show their learnings, or fill
not their mouths so full with sweetmeats, or benefices,[14]

---

[9] explicating (unfolding) (?)
[10] stain
[11] lesson
[12] anticipated
[13] clergymen
[14] ecclesiastical livings

that their tongues be not let to speak[15] truth; for that is their duty and office, except I with many other be much deceived.

Playing at cards and tables[16] is somewhat more tolerable, only for as much as therein wit is more used, and less trust is in fortune, albeit therein is neither laudable study nor exercise. But yet men delighting in virtue might with cards and tables devise games wherein might be much solace and also study commodious: as devising a battle or contention between virtue and vice, or other like pleasant and honest invention.

The chess, of all games wherein is no bodily exercise, is most to be commended, for therein is right subtle engine[17] whereby the wit is made more sharp and remembrance quickened. And it is the more commendable and also commodious if the players have read the moralization of the chess,[18] and when they play, do think upon it. Which books be in English, but they be very scarce, because few men do seek in plays for virtue or wisdom.

[15] prevented from speaking   [16] a game like backgammon
[17] ingenuity
[18] reference to William Caxton's *The Game and Play of the Chesse* (1476)

27

That Shooting in a Long-Bow Is Principal
of All Other Exercises

Tully[1] saith in his first book of *Offices:* "We be not to that intent brought up by nature that we should seem to be made to play and disport, but rather to gravity and studies of more estimation." Wherefore it is written of Alexander, emperor of Rome, for his gravity called *Severus,* that in his childhood, and before he was taught the letters of Greek or Latin, he never exercised any other play or game but only one, wherein was a similitude of justice; and therefore it was called in Latin *ad iudices,* which is in English, to the judges. But the form thereof is not expressed by the said author, nor none other that I have yet read. Wherefore I will repair again to the residue of honest exercise.

And for as much as Galen, in his second book of the preservation of health, declareth to be in them these qualities or diversities: that is to say, that some be done with exceeding of might, and as it were violently, and that is called valiant exercise; some with swift or hasty motion; other with strength and celerity, and that may be called vehement. The particular kinds of every of them he describeth, which were too long here to be rehearsed.

But inasmuch as he also saith that he that is of good

[1] Cicero

estate in his body ought to know the power and effect of
every exercise, but he needeth not to practice any other
but that which is moderate and mean between every ex-
tremity, I will now briefly declare in what exercise now
in custom among us may be most found of that mediocrity; and may be augmented or minished[2] at the pleasure
of him that doth exercise, without thereby appairing[3]
any part of delectation or commodity thereof. And in
mine opinion none may be compared with shooting in
the long-bow, and that for sundry utilities that come
thereof, wherein it incomparably excelleth all other exercise. For in drawing of a bow easy and congruent[4] to
his strength, he that shooteth doth moderately exercise
his arms and the over part of his body; and if his bow be
bigger, he must add to more strength, wherein is no less
valiant exercise than in any other whereof Galen writeth.

In shooting at butts, or broad arrow marks,[5] is a mediocrity of exercise of the lower parts of the body and legs,
by going a little distance a measurable pace.

At rovers or pricks,[6] it is at his pleasure that shooteth
how fast or softly he listeth[7] to go; and yet is the praise
of the shooter neither more ne[8] less, for as far or nigh the
mark is his arrow when he goeth softly as when he run-
neth.

Tennis, seldom used and for a little space, is a good
exercise for young men, but it is more violent than
shooting, by reason that two men do play. Wherefore
neither of them is at his own liberty to measure the exercise. For if the one strike the ball hard, the other that
intendeth to receive him is then constrained to use sem-

---

[2] diminished   [3] impairing
[4] suited   [5] targets
[6] butts, rovers, and pricks are variations of the archer's sport
[7] wishes   [8] nor

blable[9] violence if he will return the ball from whence it came to him. If it trill[10] fast on the ground, and he intendeth to stop—or if it rebound a great distance from him, and he would eftsoons[11] return it—he cannot then keep any measure in swiftness of motion.

Some men would say that in mediocrity, which I have so much praised in shooting, why should not bowling, clash, pins, and quoiting[12] be as much commended? Verily as for two the last be to be utterly abjected[13] of all noblemen, in like wise football, wherein is nothing but beastly fury and extreme violence; whereof proceedeth hurt, and consequently rancor and malice do remain with them that be wounded. Wherefore it is to be put in perpetual silence.

In clash is employed too little strength; in bowling oftentimes too much, whereby the sinews be too much strained and the veins too much chafed. Whereof oftentimes is seen to ensue ache or the decrease of strength or agility in the arms. Where, in shooting, if the shooter use the strength of his bow within his own tiller,[14] he shall never be therewith grieved or made more feeble.

Also in shooting is a double utility, wherein it excelleth all other exercises and games incomparably. The one is that it is, and alway hath been, the most excellent artillery for wars; whereby this realm of England hath been not only best defended from outward hostility, but also in other regions a few English archers have been seen to prevail against people innumerable; also won impregnable cities and strongholds, and kept them in the midst of the strength of their enemies. This is the feat whereby

---

[9] similar   [10] spin
[11] immediately
[12] various games of bowling or hurling
[13] rejected
[14] "the limit or measure of the strength of a bow" (Croft)

Englishmen have been most dread and had in estimation with outward[15] princes, as well enemies as allies. And the commodity thereof hath been approved as far as Jerusalem, as it shall appear in the lives of Richard the First and Edward the First, kings of England, who made several journeys to recover that holy city of Jerusalem into the possession of Christian men; and achieved them honorably, the rather by the power of this feat of shooting.

The premises considered, O what cause of reproach shall the decay of archers be to us now living! Yea, what irrecuperable damage either to us or them in whose time need of semblable defense shall happen! Which decay, though we already perceive, fear, and lament, and for the restoring thereof cease not to make ordinances, good laws, and statutes, yet who effectually putteth his hand to continual execution of the same laws and provisions, or, beholding them daily broken, winketh not at the offenders? O merciful God, how long shall we be mockers of ourselves? How long shall we scorn at our one[16] calamity, which both with the eyes of our mind and also our bodily eyes we see daily imminent, by neglecting our public weal and contemning the due execution of laws and ordinances? But I shall hereof more speak in another place, and return now to the second utility found in shooting in the long-bow: which is killing of deer, wild fowl, and other game, wherein is both profit and pleasure above any other artillery.

And verily I suppose that before cross-bows and hand guns were brought into this realm—by the sleight of our enemies, to the intent to destroy the noble defense of archery—continual use of shooting in the long-bow made the feat so perfect and exact among Englishmen that they

<hr />

[15] foreign   [16] own (?)

then as surely and soon killed such game which they listed to have as they now can do with the cross-bow or gun; and more expeditely[17] and with less labor they did it. For being therein industrious, they killed their game further from them (if they shot a great strength) than they can with a cross-bow, except it be of such weight that the arm shall repent the bearing thereof twenty years after.

Moreover in the long-bow may be shot more arrows and in less time, ne by the breaking thereof ensueth so much harm as by breaking of the cross-bow. Besides that all times in bending, the cross-bow is in peril of breaking. But this sufficeth for the declaration of shooting, whereby it is sufficiently proved that it incomparably excelleth all other exercise, pastime, or solace. And hereat I conclude to write of exercise which appertaineth as well to princes and noblemen—as to all other by their example—which determine to pass forth their lives in virtue and honesty. And hereafter, with the assistance of God, unto whom I render this mine account (for the talent that I have of him received), I purpose to write of the principal and (as I might say) the particular study and affairs of him that by the providence of God is called to the most difficult cure[18] of a public weal.

[17] readily   [18] care, charge

Libri primi finis.

JOHN M. MAJOR received his A.B. and M.A. (in Classics) from Syracuse University, and his M.A. (in English) and Ph.D. from Harvard University. From 1950 to 1953 he was instructor at Oberlin College, and from 1954 to 1957, at Duke University. He has been at the University of Colorado since 1957—as Assistant Professor of English from 1957 to 1961, as Associate Professor of English from 1961 to 1966, and as Professor of English from 1966.

Professor Major is the author of *Sir Thomas Elyot and Renaissance Humanism* (1964) and has had articles on Chaucer, Spenser, Shakespeare, and Milton published in scholarly journals.